CHINA: Pushing toward the Year 2000

by the same authors

THE CHINESE WAY

CHINA
Pushing toward the Year 2000

by Gil Loescher with Ann Dull Loescher

Illustrated with photographs

Harcourt Brace Jovanovich   New York and London

Except where indicated, the photographs that appear in this book were taken by the authors.

Pinyin spelling has been used throughout.

Requests for permission to make copies of any part of the work should be mailed to: Permissions, Harcourt Brace Jovanovich, Inc., 757 Third Avenue, New York, New York 10017.

The author wishes to thank the following for permission to quote from the sources listed below:

ALFRED A. KNOPF, INC., a division of Random House, Inc., for the excerpt on page 53 from pages 677 and 678 of *The Diplomacy of Imperialism* by William L. Langer, Vol. 2, © 1935, by the Bureau of International Research, Harvard University and Radcliffe College.

WILLIAM MORROW AND COMPANY, INC., for the excerpt on pages 104–105 from pages 174 and 177 of *Thunder Out of China* by Theodore White and Anna Lee Jacoby, © 1946, by William Sloane Associates, Inc.

PANTHEON BOOKS, a division of Random House, Inc., for the excerpts on pages 42 and 43 from pages 60 and 62 of *A Chinese View of China* by John Gittings, © 1973, by John Gittings.

THE UNIVERSITY OF CHICAGO PRESS for the excerpt on page 111 from pages 200 and 201 of *America's Failure in China* by Tang Tsou, Vol. 1, © 1963, by The University of Chicago.

Printed in the United States of America

LIBRARY OF CONGRESS CATALOGING IN PUBLICATION DATA
Loescher, Gil
China: pushing toward the year 2000
Bibliography: p. Includes index.
SUMMARY: Discusses events which led to the rise of the Chinese Communist party and outlines policies which many believe will modernize this underdeveloped agrarian country.
1. China—History—Juvenile literature. [1. China—History]   I. Loescher, Ann Dull.   II. Title.
DS736.L57   951.05   80-8802
ISBN 0-15-217506-7   AACR2

First edition B C D E

To Margaret Madeline and Claire Helen

Acknowledgments

We are grateful to our editor, Barbara Lucas, whose interest in and knowledge of China was of invaluable help to us. We would also like to thank Professor Peter Moody, Director of Asian Studies at the University of Notre Dame, for reading our manuscript with a critical eye.

Contents

Illustrations on pages 71–92

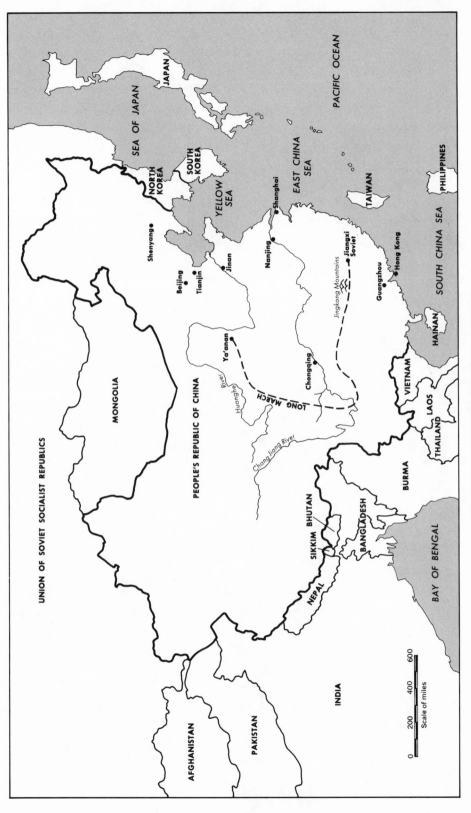

PEOPLE'S REPUBLIC OF CHINA AND SURROUNDING AREA

UNION OF SOVIET SOCIALIST REPUBLICS

MONGOLIA

PEOPLE'S REPUBLIC OF CHINA

Shenyang

Beijing
Tianjin
Jinan

Nanjing

Shanghai

Ya'anan

Huanghe River

LONG MARCH

Chongqing

Chang Jiang River

Jingkong Mountains

Jiangxi Soviet

Guangzhou

Hong Kong

AFGHANISTAN

PAKISTAN

INDIA

NEPAL

SIKKIM
BHUTAN

BANGLADESH

BURMA

THAILAND

LAOS

VIETNAM

HAINAN

BAY OF BENGAL

SOUTH CHINA SEA

TAIWAN

EAST CHINA SEA

PHILIPPINES

PACIFIC OCEAN

YELLOW SEA

SEA OF JAPAN

NORTH KOREA

SOUTH KOREA

JAPAN

0   200   400   600

Scale of miles

1

Changing China

In 1980 the giant portraits of Mao Zedong (Mao Tse-tung) and Karl Marx that had long adorned Tianan Men (Tien An Men) Square in Beijing (Peking), the symbolic center of Chinese communism, were suddenly taken down. The National People's Congress, China's legislative assembly, also met, and Hua Guofeng (Hua Kuo-feng), Mao Zedong's handpicked successor, resigned as prime minister of China. At the same time men close to Deng Xiaoping (Teng Hsiao-ping), China's vice-premier, were promoted to leadership positions. The Congress declared profits, incentives, and economic competition as official Chinese policy to encourage free enterprise and economic growth. The trial of Mao's wife, Jiang Qing (Chiang Ching), and her three radical Shanghai associates (the so-called Gang of Four) began in late 1980 and ended in 1981 with Jiang Qing being given a suspended death sentence. A formal examination of Chairman Mao's role in the past was in the making, and the fate of Communist Party Chairman Hua Guofeng hung in the balance. These new policies and shifts in leadership were taking place just four years after Mao's death in 1976. They were as sweeping as any changes that have occurred since the Chinese Communists took power in 1949. It was incredible that it all happened so quickly. However, it is clear in retrospect that several dramatic events and public protests, unusual in China in recent years, led up to these changes.

POSTER: *January 1979:* A six-foot poster appeared on Beijing's Democracy Wall. It announced that an official public meeting would be held in Tianan Men Square to discuss the direction China was taking and to "reappraise Chairman Mao." At the same time the national *People's Daily* declared that the Chinese "should not expect that every thesis and every instruction of Mao was precisely correct and perfect."

PROTEST: *January 1979:* A hundred angry Chinese peasants shouting, "We're tired of being hungry," and, "Down with oppression," tried to storm the residence of Communist Party Chairman Hua Guofeng in order to air their grievances to him.

POSTER: *January 1979:* A poster on Beijing's Democracy Wall pleads for human rights and socialist democracy as well as freedom of the press, speech, and association, stating, "We know something about America; we know of Washington, Lincoln, Jefferson, etc. We know of the Declaration of Independence and its principles of human rights. We know that human rights are very important in America and in the speeches of President Carter."

PROTEST: *February 1979:* At least 400 students marched down Beijing's main avenue to protest the admission of several students to universities because of political connections.

SIT-DOWN: *February 1979:* Shanghai Radio reported that hundreds of Chinese youths had staged a sit-down on a major railroad line. They stopped trains in and out of Shanghai for at least twelve hours. Their major demand was that they be allowed to return permanently to Shanghai from the countryside where they had been sent to work. They wanted an audience with the Shanghai authorities to discuss their grievances.

CRACKDOWN: *January 1980:* Senior Deputy Premier Deng Xiaoping called for a crackdown on freedom of expression. He urged a tightening of party discipline in China. Deng urged that China's "big four" freedoms—to speak out freely, to air views fully, to hold debates, and to write wall posters—be abolished.

CONGRESS: *September 1980:* At the National People's Congress in Beijing, Hua Guofeng yielded his position as prime minister of China to Zhao Ziyang, a protégé of Deng Xiaoping. The Congress outlawed poster criticisms such as those which appeared on Democracy Wall and declared that economic construction must come first and political ideology second.

In order to make sense of the startling changes taking place in China, it is important to develop an appreciation of China's historical experience. This is not the first time China has adopted (and adapted) Western solutions to its problems—particularly in the fields of science and technology. Nor is it surprising that the Chinese Communists experimented briefly with allowing, and even encouraging, criticism and limited demands for human rights. Popular demonstrations and protests have a long history in China. Throughout Chinese history individuals have criticized their leaders. In traditional China it was the moral responsibility of educated persons to speak out when the leaders had not treated the people fairly. Under Mao, Chinese intellectuals lashed out at Chinese Communist Party rule.

There is also in recent Chinese history a clear pattern of pendulum swings. First, there was a swing toward pragmatism and ties with the outside world. That movement was followed by an abrupt swing back toward ideological purity and a closing of the door to outside influence.

The three major political upheavals of the past three decades—the Great Leap Forward of the 1950s, the Cultural Revolution of the 1960s, and the ascendancy of the Gang of Four in the 1970s—were in fact deliberately set in motion by Mao himself. His first big campaign was the Great Leap Forward of 1958. Mao declared that economic growth was too slow and that the Chinese people in a show of mass enthusiasm should farm intensively and work around the clock in factories. It ended disastrously two years later with an exhausted labor force, ruined equipment, and wasted new materials. In the political struggles that followed, although Mao managed to oust several officials who criticized his programs, he lost his grip on the leadership.

After the Great Leap Forward, China returned to a more pragmatic industrialization program and encouraged technical and professional expertise over ideological purity. However, in an effort to recapture supreme power and to impose his own egalitarian and mass mobilization ideals, Mao turned to his wife, Jiang Qing, and the Gang of Four to launch the Cultural Revolution in 1966. He called on them to lead masses of students in Red Guard units to "bombard the headquarters" and to attack the party leaders in Beijing. The head of state, Liu Shaoqi (Liu Shao-chi), was branded the "number one capitalist roader." He was expelled from the party and later died in prison. His colleague, Deng Xiaoping, was also purged and imprisoned.

Although Mao Zedong was forced in 1969 to wind down the Cultural Revolution because of increasing disorder, its effect lingered disastrously. The Gang of Four prevented any restoration of law and order in China. Only the most rudimentary legal system existed, and bullying and injustice occurred on a massive scale.

Politics and ideology dominated all aspects of Chinese life, but the most disruptive of the Maoist programs was in the field of education. Mao and the Gang of Four opposed an emphasis on academic quality and elitist education. They argued that politics alone had to guide China's progress, or it would not be progress at all. They wanted education to meet the needs of peasants and workers and more time to be spent on practical work in communes and factories than in studying academic subjects. However, in trying to produce an egalitarian society in such a way, the Chinese seriously damaged the academic quality of their education programs. Many teachers were persecuted for being "too intellectual" and were purged. The authority of teachers was undermined, and as a result, many left their jobs or neglected their duties. Academic standards sank to very low levels. Advanced scientific study and research came virtually to a standstill. Because of the decline in educational and teaching standards, even university graduates were often poorly trained and ignorant of basic knowledge in their fields. China turned out few competent scientists and other specialists needed to help modernize its economy. The Chinese now refer to the years 1966–1976 as the "lost decade."

Both Mao Zedong and Zhou Enlai (Chou En-lai), China's two legendary leaders, died in 1976. A struggle for power followed. The radicals were headed by Mao's widow, Jiang

Qing, while the moderates were headed by Hua Guofeng.
The moderates won, and the Gang of Four, including Jiang
Qing, were arrested in late 1976.

Vice-Premier Deng Xiaoping and Communist Party
Chairman Hua Guofeng announced a new development
program known as the Four Modernizations. Agriculture,
industry, science and technology, and defense were
marked out for improvement, and foreign aid was sought.
Mao's doctrines were quietly played down by the new leaders. They complained that the Cultural Revolution reforms
had hindered the development of China's badly needed science and technology. Deng Xiaoping proclaimed that economic efficiency was more important than political purity,
and programs were needed to stimulate individual initiative. Deng had said back in 1962: "It does not matter
whether the mode of production is individual or collective.
What is essential is that it helps to increase food production.
It doesn't matter whether the cat is black or white; it is good
as long as it catches mice."

Deng realized that upgrading education was an essential
element in the success of China's modernization program.
As a result, the Maoist educational "reform" programs were
almost completely overturned. The new regime tried to
persuade its skilled elite to return to the classrooms and to
the research institutes. Academic standards were emphasized instead of political criteria. With the aim of raising the
quality of the Chinese educational system, a number of
model or key schools were developed throughout China. In
these schools, mixed-ability classes, in which the less able
were helped by the able, are gone. Key schools train the
brightest students, get the best teachers, undertake major
research projects, and set standards for first-rate academic
work for other schools in China to follow. Students are encouraged to strive for academic success, and those with tal-

ent in the arts, sciences, crafts, and sports are selected for special classes after school hours at institutes all over China, called Children's Palaces.

In addition to education, science and technology were seen by the new leadership as the crucial tools needed to regain momentum after the ten lost years of the Cultural Revolution. Whereas Mao Zedong had insisted on class struggle, mass enthusiasm, and strict egalitarianism as the means of achieving the goal of making China a "powerful, modern socialist state by the turn of the century," Deng Xiaoping emphasized production, technology, and orderly conventional approaches to achieve this goal. According to Zhou Pei-yuan, president of Beijing University, China today has only 300,000 to 400,000 scientists. In contrast, Japan, an Asian economic giant with only about one-ninth of China's population, presently has more than 500,000 scientists. In order to make up for this deficiency, Deng Xiaoping believed that it was very important to train a large number of first-rate scientists and technicians in the shortest possible time. According to Deng, this scientific elite was entitled to receive special training, to enjoy high prestige and material incentives, and even to be excused from political study. Moreover, in contrast with the self-reliance which Mao proclaimed to be a basic principle underlying China's economic development, Deng decided to turn to the outside world for extensive aid to help modernize. As a result, for the first time since the early 1950s China was actively seeking out and acquiring foreign knowledge, skills, technology, and capital.

In order for the new program to succeed, China's leaders also began to acknowledge past mistakes. For example, in mid-1980, carelessness and inefficiency in the Chinese bureaucracy caused the destruction of a Japanese-built oil rig in the Bohai Gulf off the coast of China. Apparently the petroleum industry had not bothered to translate into Chinese the Japanese operating and safety manuals. A senior official in Beijing had ordered the rig moved to a new drilling site despite warnings of a storm. The $25 million rig capsized while it was being towed, and seventy-two people aboard drowned. Several officials were jailed for their part in the disaster.

Most of the self-criticism, however, focused on the mistakes made during the last years of Mao's rule and the role played by Jiang Qing and the rest of the Gang of Four. In the eyes of China's current leaders, the most serious error of Mao and the Gang of Four was the disorder in society created through numerous ideological campaigns. Specifically, Jiang Qing was criticized for her high-handed ways, for her personal abuses of power, and for damaging economic production by preventing China's development as a modern power.

Deng Xiaoping also took steps to correct what he saw as the destructive errors of the previous leadership. For Deng the problem in China was how to restore order and confidence so that the country could modernize rapidly. It was not enough merely to stress academic excellence and the acquisition of Western science and technology. Rather, China's new leadership recognized that a degree of freedom, security, and some material incentives help motivate workers and contribute to the intellectual technical creativity needed.

For a brief period during 1978 and 1979 the government allowed various forms of protest that had been discouraged or prohibited in the past to occur without interference. Deng Xiaoping had hoped that freedom of expression would result in mass support for his program of economic modernization. Spontaneous street demonstrations, wall posters, and even underground journals flourished during the "Beijing Spring."

These abrupt changes in policy opened up a floodgate of criticism of Communist Party rule in China. And while Deng's Four Modernizations program met with widespread approval, there nonetheless arose a cry for a "fifth modernization" based upon democratic principles and respect for human rights. Angry peasants, often traveling long distances to Beijing and emboldened by the new mood of liberalization, demonstrated for more food and greater freedom. A poster on Beijing's Democracy Wall called for the abolition of censorship. Wall posters demanded not the "dictatorship of the proletariat," but genuine democracy. Chinese dissidents openly challenged the Communist rulers to put into practice what they preached when they proclaimed democracy, popular participation, and legal protection of individual rights.

The protest movement moved beyond anything the party could control. Consequently, the leadership felt threatened. For the Communist leaders, democracy did not mean freedom to criticize the Communist system or the present party leadership itself. It was not surprising, therefore, that the government reacted severely. Police arrested the most prominent Chinese dissidents and sentenced several critics, who were accused of "injuring socialism" and "opposing the interest of the people," to hard labor and long prison terms. In 1980 the right to put up wall posters was removed from the Chinese constitution. The party leadership felt the dissidents had overreacted and taken advantage of the situation, had tried to destroy the government rather than to seek reform.

At the same time Deng Xiaoping continued to liberalize the Chinese political system in order to grant the individual some protection against potential future tyrants. New legal codes were drafted in order to prevent abuse of power by the police. Many of the restrictions that had previously been placed on religious worship, contact with foreigners, and access to Western literature were lifted. For the first time since the Cultural Revolution, foreign films began being shown in Chinese cinemas, traditional operas were no longer banned, and stage performances were no longer restricted to a limited number of revolutionary ballets and operas. Western orchestral music, ballet, songs, and dances from every part of the world began being performed. Even relatively free democratic elections at commune and factory levels were promoted by the government.

In general, the present leadership is trying to foster an atmosphere in which restrictions on individuals are reduced. The idea is to encourage the Chinese people to look objectively at China's problems as the first step toward solving them. For example, in 1980 the National People's Congress called on the Chinese government to make investigative reporting easier so that newspapers can tell "the bad as well as the good and dare to disclose cases of lawbreaking among the cadres."

As the 1980s begin, however, many Chinese remain skeptical of the new reforms and laws and doubt whether they can really offer much individual freedom for the ordinary citizen. They are also unwilling to believe that all of China's difficulties are the result of the policies of the Gang of Four. Thus, the biggest problem for current Chinese Communist leadership is how to impose some limits on freedom to question China's socialism and still win back the trust of the people and get them involved in the modernization drive.

The current Chinese attempt to modernize is not an entirely new effort. The task involves the revival of a society that at the time Europe was locked into the darkness of the Middle Ages, was a great advanced civilization. Until the Industrial Revolution in the West, the Chinese were probably among the most creative and industrious people in the world. During the nineteenth and twentieth centuries the Chinese attempted to reconcile some of the most difficult conflicts of the modern age. The conflicts between egalitarianism and modernization, freedom and bureaucracy, and democracy and order have been at the root of most political debates in China. There has been, for example, a debate in China for more than a century about how the country should modernize and what role Western countries should play in this process. Nearly 100 years ago some Chinese intellectuals argued that the path to national development and strength rested on China's ability to modernize along the Western pattern of economic liberalism and parliamentary democracy. Others believed that China should rely solely on itself for economic development.

This national debate has continued into the twentieth century and up to the present time. In their desire for China to become a modern industrial nation by the year 2000, the current leaders stress the importance of economic growth. Indeed, although China is still a developing country, its economy is modern and diversified. China's industries today can make trucks, textile machinery, electronics, petrochemicals, nuclear weapons, and space satellites. However, some thoughtful Chinese wonder whether China is not moving a little too quickly and aping the West at the expense of its own culture and revolution. They wonder whether China will fall into the trap which so many other developing countries have fallen into and will industrialize at the expense of agriculture and purchase expensive and sophisticated foreign technology rather than rely on simpler technology.

In many important respects, what is happening now in China is an outgrowth of the past as well as a manifestation of the impact of present events upon it. It is to China's history and roots that we now turn for answers to the present.

2

Historical Roots

China is well known for the length and continuity of its history. The Chinese began recording their history in the eighth century B.C. at a time when about a dozen small feudal states were clustered along the basin of the Yellow River. Off and on for more than 500 years, these warring states struggled for supremacy until one feudal lord, Qin Shi Huangdi (Ch'in Shih Huang-ti), unified China in the third century B.C. He made himself emperor and established the Qin (Ch'in) dynasty. Although the Qin dynasty was short-lived, it was succeeded by the Han dynasty, which ruled the Empire for a little more than four centuries. The period of the Han dynasty was contemporary with the founding and rise to power of the Roman Empire. Its territories were fully as extensive as those of Rome. It was also a highly creative civilization in politics and culture. In addition, under the Han, the pattern of traditional Chinese rule was set. Although subsequent dynasties came and went, the political structure of the Empire remained essentially stable for the next 2,000 years.

The Chinese believed that the path to order and stability was through social organization. The emperor was at the top of the social and political order. He was known as the Son of Heaven. As such, he was considered both king and priest and the link between heaven and earth. The emperor set the calendar and supposedly intervened between his people and the forces of nature.

Just beneath the emperor on the pyramid of power were his scholar-bureaucrats, an elite group used by him to help administer the Empire. During the Han dynasty the emperors began the practice of recruiting a bureaucracy through civil service examinations. In theory, it was possible for a man of the humblest origins to rise to the highest positions in the state. All he had to do was acquire the education necessary to pass the civil service exams. However, most Chinese were too poor to afford the cost of the long years of education required to prepare for these rigorous tests. Thus, for the most part, the small minority of scholar-bureaucrats who rose to serve the emperor came from the educated class of local officials, landowners, and gentry. China's scholar-officials enjoyed great prestige and many privileges. In no other civilization did education hold so central a place or did learned men enjoy such great political authority.

Third in the ranking of social classes in China were the farmers. Although Chinese peasant farmer , often suffered from debt, taxation, forced labor, and famine, farming was always recognized as fundamentally important to the Chinese society and economy. Over 90 percent of all Chinese people were in the countryside and made their living by farming. The emperor and his court, the scholar-officials, and the peasant farmers formed the basis for the Chinese imperial system for 2,000 years.

Finally, at the very bottom of the pyramid of power in China were the merchants and soldiers. There is an old Chinese saying that one should not use good iron to make nails and should not use good men to make soldiers.

The Chinese looked upon government as an entire way of life personified in the person of the emperor. He ruled by example. He and his ministers were expected to be men with ideas and administrative skills. More important, they were expected to set proper standards for the behavior and thinking of the rest of society. They were supposed to give the people a picture of the "correct" way of life.

The importance of proper human relationships in society was stressed above all else. Within society, individuals were required to subordinate themselves to the interests of the larger community. At the heart of the web of human relationships that gave the system stability was the family. The Chinese philosopher Confucius taught that everybody should behave according to correct norms. Sons should be loyal to their fathers as subjects were loyal to their emperor. At the same time he taught that fathers should be good parents to their sons just as emperors should be good rulers to their subjects. Thus, a disobedient son was not a proper son, and a father who abused his children was not a proper father. So, too, an emperor who behaved like a tyrant was not a proper emperor. As long as everyone acted within the Confucian social framework, it was felt that order and good government would prevail.

Not everyone believed that the teachings of Confucius and his followers would give China order and stability. A group of scholar-officials called the Legalists stressed the importance of ensuring law and order through the threat of punishment. They believed that human nature was weak and that men could not be trusted to behave well. Strict laws were necessary to punish and threaten individuals who posed a threat to order. Beginning in the seventh century, criminal legal codes were adopted in China. These codes were strictly penal in nature. Individuals accused of crimes were presumed guilty and had no right to defend themselves. The use of torture to extract confessions was common. A body of civil law never developed in China.

There was no independent legal profession and judiciary as there is in Western nations today.

Historically good government in China has been perceived as government by good men rather than as government by good laws. Confucius believed that government should be the "preserve of virtuous men," and this view ruled state doctrine for most dynasties in imperial China. Confucianism and Legalism offered little room for what we know today as democracy. Consequently, there were no competing political powers. Opposition to the emperor and his court was taken as a sign of disloyalty and was punishable by death.

Nevertheless, Confucian society had many humane and democratic traits. Civil service examinations provided some social mobility and equality of opportunity. In addition, people judged their officials by the same moral standards they set for themselves and the rest of society. They did not admire unprincipled tactics, dishonest dealings, or personal luxuries on the part of the scholar-officials. The emperor even appointed imperial censors with powers to investigate charges of misrule by officials both in the capital and in the provinces. If scholar-officials were found guilty of bad rule or poor behavior, they were criticized and often driven from office.

There were also important checks on the emperor. Although it was believed that the emperor enjoyed a Mandate from Heaven to rule, this right was conditional. His reign would last only so long as his rule was good. A king who behaved as a tyrant could lose the title of emperor and be made an outlaw. If he ruled unjustly, the people had the right to revolt. As a dynasty became weak and misfortunes overtook the Empire, the conviction that the ruling family was losing the Mandate of Heaven spread among the people. Although the misfortunes might be either natural disasters, such as floods or drought, or man-made results of corruption and inefficient administration, unrest would mount. Rebels would then rise to claim the mandate. Only when a successor to the throne emerged would a new, more powerful dynasty be set up. According to a Chinese proverb, "Heaven sees as the people see; heaven hears as the people hear."

For 2,000 years the Chinese Empire conceived itself as the hub of civilization, the great school of the world, and indeed, for centuries the Chinese civilization was both spiritually and materially richer than any other. The Chinese enjoyed highly developed art, literature, and philosophy. As late as the eighteenth century, for example, China contained more books than all the other nations of the world put together. Chinese literature ranged from poetry to hair-raising tales of adventure. Chinese painting and ceramics were universal in their appeal. Chinese craftsmanship in lacquer, bronze, jade, furniture making, carpets, and silk was superb. China was the source of a classical tradition for neighboring Asian countries almost identical to the Greek and Roman tradition for European countries. Classical Chinese language and literature were as much the foundation of scholarship in Korea, Vietnam, and Japan as Greek and Latin were in Europe. China also developed political and social institutions that were superior in many ways to what had been accomplished thus far by any other people. The Chinese civil service, for example, which was begun about 200 B.C., had no equivalent in the West until the eighteenth century.

The medieval Chinese were without a doubt the most fruitfully inventive people on earth. Their major inventions include paper, silk weaving, clockworks, astronomical instruments, the horizontal loom, the spinning wheel, and the waterwheel. Their inventions were fundamental developments in the history of man as toolmaker. As Mao Zedong reminded his countrymen:

> The compass was invented in China very long ago. . . . The art of papermaking was discovered as early as 1800 years ago. Block printing was invented 1300 years ago. In addition, movable types were invented 800 years ago. Gunpowder was used in China earlier than in Europe. China, with a recorded history of almost four thousand years, is therefore one of the oldest civilizations in the world.

Even more surprising is the fact that until first the Renaissance and later the Industrial Revolution in Europe, China was superior to the West in science and technology. Not many people realize that Western superiority in technology is a fairly recent phenomenon. What we know as modern science began in Europe in the sixteenth and seventeenth centuries. Many people assume that all technology developed in Western culture; in fact, many scientific and technological developments had their origins in China centuries ago. For example, the Chinese mastered the technique of making cast iron centuries before the Europeans. Although the use of cast iron is considered one of the foundations of Western civilization, there was no cast iron in Europe until about A.D. 1380, when blast furnaces in Germany and the Low Countries started to make it. The Chinese, however, had been making cast-iron agricultural tools in the second century B.C. There are many other outstanding examples of how far ahead of the West China was until the Renaissance and the Industrial Revolution. It has recently come to light that a water-powered blowing engine designed by Wang Zhen (Wang Chen) about A.D. 1300 was the first engine to use a combination of eccentric, connecting rod, and piston rod. This engine predates both Leonardo da Vinci's and James Watt's designs. Thus, it was a Chinese inventor who first introduced the principles basic to the internal-combustion engine. Chinese engineers were also ahead of their Western counterparts in bridge and canal building and in irrigation and water management.

It is significant, however, that technological innovation in China did not lead to an industrial revolution as it did in the West. The social changes that occurred in the West as a result of the Industrial Revolution were directly tied to capitalism. To a great extent, the amount of profit to be made from an invention or innovation determined the advancement of its technology. In China, however, technology was not permitted to bring about radical social changes.

The chief reason for this lack of change may have been the bureaucratic and feudal system of traditional China. Floods, droughts, and pestilence swept China throughout its history, often killing millions in a single year. Drought and flood—the primary causes of famine—were held at bay by systems of canals, reservoirs, embankments, and irrigation works. The waterworks were under local control, but central planning was required for national security. In particular, under benevolent dynasties, the Chinese civil service maintained grain surpluses to ward off famine in bad harvest years. However, the price paid for this security was a rigidly controlled Chinese society.

Wealth was concentrated in the hands of a small number of people. Civil servants jealously guarded their position and privilege against change. The bureaucracy was so successful that it inhibited the rise of Chinese merchants to power in the state. It strictly controlled merchant guilds, and it prevented individuals from accumulating much capital. The state heavily taxed all mining enterprises and after the fifteenth century prohibited sea trade and expansion. There was no incentive for an individual to use technology to improve his lot because rising in the society outside of the established patterns was out of the question. The best brains from all levels of society went into the civil service. Stability and order, not individual competition, were the keys to good society and a sound government. Thus, many inventions may have originated in China, but only in the more competitive and dynamic West did science and technology bring widespread change.

Chinese civilization developed in complete isolation for a very long period. Formidable geographical barriers secluded China from close contact with other civilizations. To the north of China is the arid plateau of Mongolia and Manchuria; to the east is the sea; to the west are Tibet and the Himalayas, the highest mountains in the world; to the south are the thick tropical jungles of Vietnam and Laos. Consequently, to the Chinese, China was the world. It was populated by the Han, a black-haired people whose civilization defined the limits of the world. The Chinese Empire produced everything its people wanted. Other people were recognized to exist, but they were outsiders and believed to be of inferior culture.

In their isolated environment Chinese thought of their Empire as the center of the civilized world. Indeed, the Chinese word for China, *Zhongguo (Chung Kuo)*, means "Middle Kingdom" or "Central Country." For much of its history, China had no links with people at a similar level of development. Hence, the Chinese had no reason to doubt their claim to being the most important people in the world.

About the first or second century B.C. the Chinese finally began to make contact with western Asia, India, and even the Roman Empire. The beginnings of a caravan route across Central Asia to Persia and to the outer fringes of the Roman Empire were established, but distances were so great that the journey was equal to traveling to the moon today. Therefore, the contact with the West had no political significance. It did not in any way change Chinese life or the Chinese view of the world. The absence of any prolonged contact with a rival civilization was a factor that contributed powerfully to the traditional Chinese view of the world.

The Chinese view of relations between states was based on the idea of the Confucian social hierarchy. China stood at the center of the human family, and all other countries occupied inferior positions around it. The status and prestige of other peoples varied according to their readiness to accept Chinese culture. Even China's conquerors, such as Genghis Khan, soon learned that they could not rule the country without adopting Chinese ways to some extent. Over time, the Chinese civilized their nomadic conquerors and came to control them. In the end, the Mongols from the north adopted Chinese ways and the Chinese language.

Beyond China, in roughly concentric zones, lay regions of differing importance and interest to the Chinese. Those countries immediately surrounding China, such as Vietnam, Korea, and Japan, were most important. They accepted Chinese culture and modeled themselves on Chinese institutions and civilization. They accepted the Chinese system of writing, the tenets of Confucianism, and the family system. They acknowledged Chinese superiority by periodically sending tribute missions to the Chinese court. In most cases these tributary states were left to rule themselves as they liked without Chinese interference. Beyond these neighboring peoples were Persia, India, and other Asian countries which were relatively well known to the Chinese. Beyond these countries lay all the rest of the world. The Chinese knew little or nothing about these peoples and considered them all "barbarians."

When Europeans began to make contact with the Chinese in the eighteenth century, they, too, were regarded as inferior. Westerners, like all foreigners, were expected to acknowledge their inferiority and tributary status publicly. Their representatives were expected to kowtow before the emperor in the traditional manner. This meant they were to genuflect three times and prostrate themselves nine times in a humiliating, if not a physically difficult, maneuver. No matter how loudly Westerners protested, no matter how unreasonable they found the Chinese system, they were to receive the same treatment as all other inferior tribute-bearing nations.

When King George III of England sent his emissary Lord Macartney to the Chinese court in 1792 to request that relations between England and China be put on equal footing, he was sternly rebuffed. The Chinese emperor sent this message back to London: "Our celestial Empire possesses all things in prolific abundance and lacks no products within its borders. There is therefore no need to import the manufacture of outside barbarians in exchange for our own produce." Emperor Qian Long (Ch'ien Lung) wanted no part of a system of international intercourse which implied that any distant ruler was an equal. China was the Middle Kingdom, the center of the universe. The British king could do no better than to earn the benevolence of the Chinese emperor. Thus, a source of irreconcilable conflict existed between China and the rapidly expanding Western powers.

3

Early Encounters
with the West

In the early eighteenth century the political and social structure of the Chinese Empire was essentially stable. China was ruled by the Manchus, who had established the Qing (Ch'ing) dynasty in the seventeenth century. The emperor, aided by the scholar-officials, controlled the government. He ruled by the Mandate of Heaven, and his edicts had the authority of a priest-king. His vast realm stretched from the Gobi desert to the tropics; it included all of China proper, Manchuria, Mongolia, Xinjiang (Sinkiang), and Tibet, and it was known as "everything under heaven." The bordering areas of Korea, Vietnam, Burma, and Nepal were tribute-bearing countries.

By the late eighteenth century, however, China had been invaded by explorers, traders, and missionaries who came around the Cape of Good Hope, across the Indian Ocean, and through the Strait of Malacca and the South China Sea. The Chinese did not invite these adventurers from Portugal, Holland, Britain, France, and Spain who first appeared along its south coast and were soon followed by seafaring captains from America.

These men came in search not of the culture of the East, but of the materials and markets of the East. In short, they came seeking their fortunes. Long-distance travel was a risky business. The sea journey to China was hazardous, and the odds of a safe return were at best even. Consequently, adventurers, who were not the most learned or cultivated of men, made most of these early trips to China.

They had had their imaginations fired by early accounts of the vast riches of China. Marco Polo and other overland travelers had reached the court of the great khan who ruled China in the thirteenth century. They portrayed "ancient Cathay" as a land of great material prosperity. What caught the imagination of Marco Polo was the size and splendor of Chinese cities and the material prosperity of the court. Prone to great exaggeration, he described the Chinese city of Hangzhou (Hangchow) in his journal as having "twelve thousand bridges of stone, for the most part so lofty that a great fleet could pass beneath them." Polo also gave a greatly exaggerated account of the magnificence of the great khan's court. According to Polo's account, among the presents the ruler customarily received at the New Year were 100,000 richly adorned white horses.

Although Polo spent a long time in China, he never mentioned in his journals any of the defects of the Chinese system. In fact, as in Europe at that time, poverty stood in naked contrast with the great luxury of the court and the scholar-official class. Disease flourished. In bad years natural disasters and famine were frequent.

Idyllic and oversimplified views of China were continued by the Jesuit priests, led by Matteo Ricci, who lived in China during the seventeenth and eighteenth centuries. Just as the vision of China as fabulously prosperous was a result of the reports of Marco Polo, the portrayal of China as a strong, united, and happy state governed by a benevolent despot in accordance with the moral precepts of the wise sage Confucius derives partially from the Jesuits. Ignored or played down were the corrupt and divisive features of Chinese society, such as the wicked influence at court of powerful eunuchs, the ill-treatment of minority peoples, and the numerous peasant rebellions. The image of China given to the outside world by these early Western visitors was that of a flowery land dotted with stately palaces and inhabited by a permanently smiling and prosperous people. This was an image which closely resembled the design on the famous blue willow pattern plate!

European and American images of China were deeply colored by these early accounts. In many ways, Westerners were as ill informed about China as the Chinese were about them. Our Founding Fathers had heard of China as the ancient kingdom of Cathay. They had heard that it possessed a great culture devoted to the arts and sciences and had invented such things as paper, gunpowder, and the compass. They had heard that it was ruled according to the ethical teachings of the Chinese sage Confucius. However, the seafaring explorers and traders were not prepared for what they would encounter once they established actual contact with the Chinese. For example, none of the early Western adventurers knew anything of the Chinese language. Chinese culture was totally alien to the visiting Westerners in the eighteenth century. To begin with, even simple everyday things seemed backward. The Chinese had their first names last and their last names first; they ate soup in place of dessert; they made a gesture that looked like "come here" when they meant "good-bye." The Western adventurers were further amazed by what they saw: men with pigtails, women with bound feet, ancestor worship, female infanticide, child marriage, and a host of other practices which seemed strange or inhuman to most Westerners. No wonder Westerners came to regard the Chinese as peculiar and inferior.

Western explorers and traders were also unprepared for the unfriendly reception the Chinese government gave them. To the Chinese, they seemed intrusive, hairy, and bad-smelling. It should have come as no surprise, therefore, that when Westerners began to arrive in large numbers in search of quick profits, China severely restricted their commercial and other activities. Chinese officials did condescend to permit Westerners, including Americans, to engage in trade, but only at the port of Guangzhou (Canton) on the south coast of China and only under strict conditions. Western merchants were allowed to do business only along the banks of the river outside the Guangzhou city walls; they were not allowed within the walls at all. Nor were they allowed any direct contact with high Chinese officials. Instead, trade was conducted through a group of Chinese merchants called the Cohong. The Cohong had a monopoly on foreign trade and was responsible for the good conduct of the foreign merchants. Naturally Westerners found these trading conditions extremely irritating. But the Chinese were not really interested in foreign trade. They held their own merchants to be a contemptible lower class, and foreign trade had traditionally been restricted to the bringing of tribute from vassal states to the Chinese emperor.

Unused to being treated as inferiors, Westerners were unhappy with this situation. They were also anxious to expand their trading opportunities in China. To Westerners, with their concept of an international community of equal sovereign states, the refusal of the Chinese to enter into relations with other governments on an equal basis seemed arrogant and unnecessary. The Western powers were determined to gain diplomatic access to Beijing and commercial access to more Chinese ports. China, however, was equally determined to fend them off and regarded Western demands for equal treatment as preposterous.

The drive to expand trade with China was led by the British. With the Industrial Revolution in the West, the British began to seek sources of raw materials for their factories and markets for their goods. In this age of Western expansion, the British navy ruled the oceans. Of all the countries of East Asia it was China that the British found most alluring. It was the biggest and richest, and it seemed to hold promise of large profits for traders. Thus, British merchants were determined to open China up.

For some time Britain had imported tea, silk, and porcelain from China. Because there was no corresponding demand for Western goods in China, the British were forced to pay for the Chinese exports with silver. The British were upset with this drain of silver from their country's coffers. This balance of payments problem continued until the 1780s when the British East India Company discovered that opium, which had been grown in India for centuries, could be sold in China at handsome prices. As greater and greater numbers of Chinese became addicted to this drug, the balance of payments was gradually reversed. Opium soon constituted half of China's imports. Silver flowed out of China at an alarming rate, and the health of the Chinese nation was seriously damaged.

These conditions prevailed for some fifty years until 1839. Then, alarmed that opium traffic in China had gotten completely out of control, the Chinese emperor decided to put a sudden end to it. In the autumn of that year the emperor's commissioner Lin Ze-Xu (Lin Tse-hsu) sent a stern protest to Queen Victoria. He appealed to her conscience to stop the opium trade, and thinking that tea and rhubarb were essential to Britain, he threatened to impose an embargo on these items. However, the protest went unheeded. Western merchants, still angry because of the continued unfair restrictions placed upon them by the Chinese, continued the opium trade at the port of Guangzhou. Finally, the emperor banned completely the import and smoking of opium in China. He also ordered Commissioner Lin to blockade British ships at Guangzhou and to destroy their opium. The tension between East and West reached its climax when Commissioner Lin boarded a merchant vessel and dumped foreign-owned opium worth $10 million into Guangzhou Harbor.

The British interpreted this seizure and destruction of opium as interference with their freedom of trade and as an act of aggression. As a result, British forces attacked the port of Guangzhou. The Chinese forts fell easily, even though the British had dispatched only a small expeditionary force. The Chinese army was pitifully inadequate, and its arms were no match for those of the British. Consequently, the famous so-called Opium War was little more than a skirmish and ended in disgrace for China.

The Treaty of Nanjing (Nanking) that concluded the war was a great humiliation for China. The Chinese were forced to open not only Guangzhou but four other Chinese ports— Xiamen (Amoy), Ningbo (Ningpo), Fuzhou (Foochow), and Shanghai—to British trade. Moreover, Britain required China to pay a heavy indemnity to cover the costs of the destroyed opium. In addition, China had to cede the island of Hong Kong to Britain. Other Western nations took advantage of this situation to conclude similar treaties on behalf of their merchants. For example, at the time the Treaty of Nanjing was being signed, an American sea captain, Commodore Lawrence Kearny of the *Constellation,* was anchored in Guangzhou. The captain immediately demanded from China that "the trade and commerce of the United States be placed upon the same footings as the nation most favored." This demand was granted, and shortly thereafter, in 1844, the first American emissary to China, Caleb Cushing, arrived with gunboats to sign a Chinese-American treaty. France also forced on the Chinese a treaty which provided for freedom of movement for missionaries in China. These unfair treaties abolished once and for all the traditional use of tribute as a way of doing business.

China could no longer be secluded from contact with the West. The Opium War, which was the first violent encounter between China and a Western nation, came as a terrible shock to the Chinese. Its negotiators were simply defenseless in the face of Western guns. Europeans and Americans had opened China by force. The Western barbarians were now in Chinese ports as a matter of right which they had the power to enforce.

Over the next half century Japan and Russia joined the Western nations in scrambling for political and economic advantages in China. Some fifty unequal treaties were imposed on China during this period. Each one added to China's woes. China lost more territories or claims to territories, including Qiulung (Kowloon), the maritime provinces, the Amur Valley, mountain passes in Central Asia, the Ryukyu Islands, Vietnam, Sikkim, Burma, Tibet, Macao, Formosa, and Korea. More Chinese ports and inland waterways were opened to foreign trade. The opium trade was legalized.

Over the years Westerners created a world of their own within China. They built strongly fortified compounds in major cities along the China coast, in the Chang Jiang (Yangtze) Valley, and in Manchuria. The presence of consulates, banks, clubhouses, hotels, warehouses, and Christian churches marked the privileged position of the white man in China. The Chinese people became second-class citizens in their own country. Foreigners, with their privileges, were better treated by the Chinese government than its people. In particular, foreigners enjoyed the right of extraterritoriality, or immunity from Chinese law. Foreigners who committed crimes in China were tried not in

Chinese courts, but in courts presided over by Western judges. Foreigners also controlled Chinese tariffs. By the "most favored nation" clause, every privilege China granted to one nation was automatically extended to all. Finally, missionaries also were under the protection of foreign powers. If missionaries suffered injury at the hands of the Chinese people, the powers demanded reparation from the Chinese government. The maltreatment of missionaries was often made the pretext for excessive territorial and political exactions. And in the midst of all this injustice Western gunboats waited in Chinese harbors to deal with any and all problems.

Perhaps nothing better illustrates the plight of the Chinese people at the hands of the West than the booming Chinese "coolie" trade of the mid nineteenth century. Coolies were unskilled Chinese laborers hired for subsistence wages. Thousands of Chinese were shanghaied, or kidnapped, for labor in the rubber and tin plantations of Java and the Malacca Strait, the sugar plantations of Cuba and the West Indies, and the gold mines and railroads of California and the American West. Emigration brokers in the Chinese treaty ports grew rich on the trade. So did the foreign owners who transported the coolies. The conditions of their transport to their new workplaces were horrendous. A Chinese commission sent to investigate the coolie traffic to Cuba described the sorry plight of Chinese coolies: "Eight tenths of the entire number declared that they had been kidnapped; that the mortality rate during the voyage from wounds caused by blows, suicide and sickness exceeded ten percent; that on arrival in Havana they were sold into slavery." The commission report continued:

> . . . the large majority became the property of sugar planters;
> . . . the labor on the sugar plantations is shown to be excessively

severe, and the food to be insufficient; the hours of labor are too long. . . . During the past years a large number have been killed by blows, have died from the effects of wounds; and have hanged themselves, cut their throats, poisoned themselves with opium, and thrown themselves into wells and sugar cauldrons.

The only hope for the coolies was that they might eventually serve out the terms of their contract and be given their freedom to return home to China. According to the commission, however, this was not very often the case:

On the termination of the contracts, the employers, in most cases, withhold the certificates of completion and insist on renewal of engagements . . . if the Chinese refuse to assent, they are taken to the railroad depots in chains, and watched by guards, they are forced to repair roads, receiving no compensation for their labor, undergoing a treatment exactly similar to that of criminals in jail . . . A return home, and an attempt to gain a livelihood independently, become impossible.

In California, Chinese coolies were similarly exploited and discriminated against. Although these Chinese freely emigrated to America, they were treated as inferior beings. They competed for jobs with Irish immigrants and native Californians. Orientals got jobs, it was said, because of their "subhuman" ability to exist on wages of a few cents per day. Vigilantes resorted to jungle law and lynchings to keep the "wily Orientals" in their place. The coolies were beaten and stoned, their pigtails were cut off, and dozens of them were killed in mob violence. By 1882 demands for ending Chinese immigration had become so powerful that the U.S. Congress determined to bar all Chinese. The Chinese Exclusion Act of that year placed Chinese in a unique legal category. Along with imbeciles, paupers, and prostitutes, they were refused the right to immigrate or to become American citizens.

By the mid to late nineteenth century Westerners had begun to see China as a "backward" nation. What had been admiration for a superior culture quickly changed to disdain for a backward and subhuman people. The formerly respected Chinese became "Chinamen" and "Chinks." No longer did Westerners look enviously to the East. The Chinese became "teeming faceless millions" and godless heathens. In a later era, Dr. Fu Manchu would become the sinister, slant-eyed villain in spine-chilling adventure stories. China came to represent the quintessence of incompetence among nations. Its only salvation lay in its conversion to Christianity and the adoption of the civilization of the West.

Americans, in particular, lost respect for Chinese civilization. The Americans of the nineteenth century had a very special view of the world, together with a self-image that is hard for us to remember or comprehend now. Americans believed they had a special message for mankind and were specially assigned by God, nature, or history to promote good in a world that was essentially evil. They believed in egalitarian democracy and in government that would promote the enterprise of the individual without hindering him or her. Americans also fervently believed that their free enterprise system promised a superior way of life both materially and spiritually. Holding these beliefs, Americans were very expansionist and often self-righteous.

To Americans, the Chinese almost seemed like people from another world. Everything about the two societies was different. For a long time Americans had a seemingly unlimited frontier into which men might move to escape the old society and to create a new world for themselves. Then, with the closing of the North American frontier late in the nineteenth century came a new form of expansion overseas. Americans believed in creativity and progress, the power of science, the power of the individual will, and the virtues of competition. The national myth was of a steady climbing upward into power and prosperity, both by the individual and by the country as a whole. Americans tended to ignore history and believed in change and progress as the only salvation for mankind.

The Chinese, on the other hand, venerated tradition above all else. The very notions of competition, individualism, and change were anathema to them. For the Chinese, the sense of limitation and enclosure was as much a part of individual life as of the life of the nation. Unlike America, China was not blessed with a seemingly unlimited physical space, for in spite of its enormous size, only a small percentage of the land is arable. To accumulate wealth meant to deprive the rest of the community of land, to fatten oneself while one's neighbor starved. Consequently, to the Chinese the accumulation of great wealth was antisocial. It was not a sign of success, but rather a sign of selfishness. The stress in China was on collective good and social harmony, not on individualism and competition. Also, the Chinese were directed toward the past, not the future. The educated elite focused all their scholarship on a perfect repetition of the past rather than on invention and progress.

The Americans, brimming with self-confidence, began to regard China as a country that needed their help and expertise. This was a country that needed American aid and teaching to rescue it from its downward spiral. American merchants and soldiers were followed by missionaries eager to make new converts. At the same time teachers began to arrive to set up high schools and colleges. Engineers came to chart territory, and doctors to heal the sick. The Chinese were faced with representatives from an expanding and progressive civilization whose purpose was to lift China out of the doldrums and make it a little America.

Many Chinese found these activities galling and humiliating. Old feelings of cultural superiority and pride were slow to die. Therefore, China initially resisted these encroachments. It was forced by its military weakness to admit the foreign traders to more ports and to allow the foreign missionaries to preach at will throughout the land. However, the Chinese government continued to obstruct, delay, and frustrate the provisions of the unequal treaties. The Chinese believed that if they made initial concessions to satisfy the Westerners' thirst for trade, they could eventually domesticate and control these barbarians. It was assumed that in time Westerners would accept the virtues of Chinese culture and acknowledge the superiority of the emperor, as all previous barbarian conquerers had done.

This attitude could not be upheld for long though. The treaty ports and the foreign quarters were constant reminders of Chinese weakness and the source of profound resentment against the West. The Chinese people developed a hatred of foreigners which erupted from time to time in riots, murders, and massacres. Because of its subservience to the West, the Chinese government had lost face in the eyes of its own people and could no longer control these spontaneous uprisings.

No single event in the nineteenth century so shook China as the Taiping Rebellion, which occurred between 1850 and 1864. The Taiping movement was led by men who were strongly influenced by Christian teaching and who believed themselves to be prophets of a new faith. The Taipings were determined to eradicate the most basic elements of traditional Chinese society, including the scholar-officials and the Confucian ethos on which their authority rested. The rebellion began with a small band of idealistic young revolutionaries but grew to involve tens of thousands of angry Chinese. It frightened the ruling elite and almost caused the downfall of the Manchu dynasty. Although the Taiping Rebellion was not a strictly antiforeign movement, foreigners feared that a new China might emerge to threaten their privileges. Thus, they cast their lot with the Manchu dynasty and helped the emperor quell the revolution.

With the defeat of the Taipings it seemed that the Manchus had been given a reprieve. For the time being the traditional order had triumphed. But the Taiping Rebellion had sent a shock wave through China. It was evident that the Chinese people had begun to lose confidence in the superiority of their system. Defeat at the hands of Westerners, the loss of territory to foreigners, and internal rebellions seemed to toll the death knell for traditional China.

The foreign invasions of the nineteenth century had produced a profound cultural shock for the Chinese. Westerners were people with a new technology who could not be dealt with by traditional means. They would not act as tribute bearers. Nor would they recognize the superiority of the emperor and his Empire. They could not be kept at a distance and handled by the provincial authorities. They demanded central representation and recognition as powers equal to China. The strategy of pitting one of the Western powers against the others had only limited success, for they were likely in a crisis to combine forces with the single objective of extracting further concessions from China. The Opium War and the Taiping Rebellion rocked imperial China but did not deliver the *coup de grâce.* The Chinese leaders, retaining supreme trust in their ancient system, could not bring themselves to attempt radical reform. It took another fifty years of failure, humiliation, and defeat before China could see itself clearly in relation to the rest of the world.

China's Response to the West

The Western invasion of China affected all levels of society. The presence of Western gunboats and soldiers demonstrated to all the inability of the imperial house to protect its subjects. Moreover, the evidence of new machines and manufactured goods revealed the disparity of wealth between the West and the East. Among the scholar-officials there was a more profound reaction. The Western presence and dominance challenged their belief in the superior moral basis of the Chinese culture. However, while the old order had been clearly discredited, there was great reluctance to abandon the centuries-old Chinese traditions.

Arguments over what should be done to meet the Western challenge raged for decades. Two schools of thought evolved. Conservatives believed that a great effort should be made to strengthen the dynasty, recover China's ancient power, and use that power to expel the foreigners. In the view of the proponents of this argument, the foreigner brought only evil to China; therefore, nothing Western should be accepted or used. The old ways of China, tried and trusted for so many centuries, would suffice, provided that they were directed by men of Confucian training and principles. Another school argued that only minor changes needed to be made. If Western technical skills, particularly military skills and weapons, were acquired, the foreigners could be hurled out, and China could proceed on the basis of its unchanging principles. Both schools had their followings, but those who wished to use foreign weapons and Western technology to strengthen China's ability to defend itself eventually won the struggle.

These reformers were called the Self-Strengthening Movement. Their most prominent spokesman was Zeng Guofan (Tseng Kuo-fan). He was a scholar in the Confucian tradition, highly acclaimed by his countrymen, who served for many years as viceroy of Central China. Like his countrymen, Zeng saw the West as a threat rather than as a model which China should follow. However, there were some things about the West—its military strength and the wealth and national power which flowed from that strength—that Zeng did see as desirable. Therefore, he established small arsenals to manufacture Western types of weapons and a shipyard for the construction of modern warships. He also proposed that a number of young Chinese be sent abroad to study Western technology.

It soon became apparent, though, that more than the mere acquisition of weapons would be needed to overcome China's deficiencies. The country needed to bring about modernization in order to deter the West effectively. To modernize, China needed radically to reform its institutions, its system of administration and education, and its industry. But its scholar-official class and ruling elite had a vested interest in the old way and the traditional order. They were very reluctant to adopt modern technology and resisted these early attempts at reform. Thus, for example, China's rulers were opposed to the building of railways. They felt that railways and improved communications would only make foreign invasions easier. They saw no value in industrial development and so were opposed to mining enterprises. As a result, the development of railroads

and mining in China was to fall almost completely into foreign hands, making China even more dependent on foreign powers.

While China was struggling to hold the West at arm's
length and to preserve its political and cultural independence, Japan was transforming itself into a great Asian power. Unlike the Chinese, the Japanese did not regard
themselves as the only civilized people in the world. Like
the Chinese, the Japanese disliked foreign incursions and
felt threatened by the West. But they learned from the
source that threatened them. Japan avidly adopted and
adapted much from the West. Soon after their early contacts with the West the Japanese set out to learn what made
the intruders strong in weapons, science, and technology.
They sent students abroad to learn Western methods. They
built factories and railways, reorganized their army and
navy on Western models, created a new currency and
banking system, began a merchant marine, and set up tele-
graph lines and a postal network. They framed a constitution with a diet, or parliament, and a cabinet. They
developed an educational system that copied much of what
they found in Europe and the United States. Western culture and religion were still considered disruptive of public
order and morality and so were ignored. In this way, Japan
was able to revolutionize itself without jettisoning its basic
institutions.

While Japan made itself strong, Western powers continued to nibble away at the borders of China. France moved
into Vietnam and Cambodia and threatened China's south-
west frontiers. Britain conquered Burma, and the Russians
expressed an interest in parts of Manchuria and Xinjiang.
The Japanese also became expansionist and made an omi-
nous advance on China's periphery. Moving into territories
over which China had some claim, Japan extended its rule

to the Ryukyu Islands in the 1870s. Soon afterward the Japanese began to threaten Chinese claims to Korea. Continued friction between Japan and China led to the outbreak of war in Korea in 1894.

The smaller but better-armed Japanese fleet handily defeated the Chinese fleet off the mouth of the Yalu River. Japan's new naval and military superiority over China was a result of the fact that it had modernized its entire state system on Western lines. China had resisted fundamental change and in so doing had exposed itself to further encroachment at the hands of foreigners. Once in control of Korea, Japan moved to establish a foothold on the Asian mainland at Port Arthur in Manchuria.

The Chinese suffered a humiliating defeat at the hands of the Japanese. China, the Middle Kingdom and the center of the tribute system, was humbled before Japan. This was a greater blow to Chinese pride than had been inflicted by the wars with the West.

The Western powers stopped Japan from making an inroad into their own interests in China. But their price to China was high. In return for their assistance, the Western states began carving out for themselves leaseholds and spheres of influence throughout China. The foreign powers began what was known as the scramble for concessions. China was like a ripe melon with each power hungrily slicing a huge piece. The British established themselves in the Chang Jiang Valley; the French, in South China; the Germans, in Shandong (Shantung) Province; and the Russians, in Manchuria.

The quest for concessions by the European powers worried American business interests, which feared that they might be excluded from China altogether. The American policy had been not to use force in China, but to wait until another power acted and then demand what everyone else got by invoking the most-favored-nation clause. However, by the 1890s pressures had built up for a more active United States Far Eastern policy. The end of the American frontier had been announced in 1890. Fearing that their own country had been filled up, Americans began to look overseas for trade and other activities. Thus it was that the United States began a period of expansion in the Pacific.

The American war with Spain over Cuba in 1898 was accompanied by separate moves to take over Hawaii and part of the Samoan island outposts in the Pacific. The United States took over the Philippines from Spain as well. Thus, the United States gained a strong foothold in the Far East in the same period when the imperialist powers of Europe were struggling to get their spheres of influence in different Chinese provinces. At the same time the American secretary of state John Hay wanted to protect U.S. economic and commercial interests in China. He disliked the selfish way in which European nations had marked out exclusive little patches of China for themselves. In 1900 Hay convinced the other powers to agree to an open door policy. All nations would be able to trade with China on equal terms. The open door let everyone, especially the United States, into China.

The Chinese government had not been consulted on the dismemberment of its empire. The Chinese had lost the mastery of their own home and were powerless to prevent the scramble. At the same time floods in South China and droughts in North China threatened the very survival of the dynasty. This was particularly true in 1877 and 1878, when famine took the lives of an estimated 12 million people. Defeat and loss of territory at the hands of foreigners, internal revolts, and natural disasters seemed to spell doom for traditional China.

For the first time in history the Chinese began to take a long look at themselves and to question the whole Confucian system. The strategy of gradual reform while keeping the Chinese traditions and values obviously had not worked as a means of dealing with external threats. What good was the past if it could not even protect China against Japan? Moreover, as in previous times of oppression and famine, conditions were ripe for rebellion against the Manchu dynasty. The situation called for radical measures.

The young emperor Guang Xu (Kuang Hsu) was eager to save his realm. One of his more reform-minded officials, Kang Youwei (K'ang Yu-wei), appealed to him in 1895 to institute a number of radical changes to revitalize China. Kang warned the emperor:

> If Your Majesty will not decide, or will prefer to remain in the old grooves of the Conservatives, then your territories will be swallowed up, your limbs will be bound, your viscera will be cut up, and Your Majesty will scarcely manage to retain your throne or to rule over more than a fragment of your ancient Empire.

Kang warned that unless China modernized and developed firepower to use to expel the Westerners, "she would sink in the earth, be buried in ruins, burst like an egg, and be torn into shreds." At the very thought of this, Kang said he was so angry that his "hair stood on end, his eyes stared out of their sockets, and he was not able to endure it for a single day." Finally, in 1898, Kang Youwei and some others of like mind won the ear and the support of the emperor. For 100 days in 1898, a stream of reforming decrees was issued by the emperor Guang Xu. He instituted an annual budget and abolished the practice of official sinecures. The old classical examination system was to be replaced by one which included the study of science and of foreign government. A new system of primary, secondary, and technical schools was planned.

The emperor's reforms marked the high point of the movement to defeat the foreigners by learning foreign skills. But the 100-day reform aroused the opposition of those who had a vested interest in the old ways. Conservative officials rallied around the emperor's aunt, Dowager Empress Cixi (Tzu Hsi), in a coup d'état. The emperor was seized by guards and taken to a palace on a small island in the middle of the lake in the Imperial City in Beijing. His scholar-officials were banished or beheaded, and the dowager empress assumed control of the government. The short-lived reforms came to an abrupt end. Although the old empress nurtured a fierce hatred for Westerners, she offered no realistic challenge to their incursions. Instead, when the challenge did come, it was in an outburst of violence directed against foreigners.

At about the time of the dowager empress's takeover, a popular movement, known as the Fists of Righteous Harmony, began to flare up in North China. This secret society was popularly known as the Boxers. Its members were held together by a common hatred of Westerners. They were particularly resentful of Western interference in indigenous customs, and they took the lead in attacking missionaries, diplomats, and merchants. The Boxers claimed that magic oaths and potions made them immune from bullets and other modern weapons. Encouraged by this claim to invulnerability, hundreds of thousands of Chinese peasants joined forces with the Boxers. The dowager empress hesitated to suppress the Boxer movement because she saw in it an opportunity to win popular support and to attack the foreign position in China.

In the early months of 1900 the Boxers swept across the

countryside of North China, burning and looting missionary settlements and slaughtering thousands of Chinese
Christians. Boxer ranks were swelled by mobs of destitute
vagrants who had been driven off their lands by famine,
flood, and drought. By spring, Beijing had been encircled
by fanatical bands of zealots who had the objective of driving all the barbarians into the sea. To protect themselves
from the inevitable onslaught of the Boxers, Westerners re-
inforced their legations in Beijing and prepared for the
worst. Finally, in June 1900, the Boxers burst into Beijing,
assassinated the German and the Japanese ministers, and
laid siege to foreign legations. The dowager empress chose
to remain inactive, thereby giving silent encouragement to
the rebellion.

The "Siege of Beijing" ended two months later, when an
international expeditionary force, including units from the
American Fifteenth Infantry, fought its way from the port
of Tianjin (Tientsin) overland to Beijing. En route the Westerners devastated the countryside, looting and killing in revenge for the Boxers' actions. The German kaiser told his
troops that he wanted the Chinese to tremble "for the next
thousand years" whenever they heard German spoken.
Americans participated wholeheartedly in this revenge. An
American field artillery battery smashed open one of the
gates to Beijing, and an American bugler ran up the U.S.
flag on Beijing's walls. Much of Beijing was looted, and
thousands of its inhabitants either committed suicide or
were slaughtered. The dowager empress and her court
were driven into exile.

After suppressing the Boxer uprising, the foreign powers
imposed a harsh settlement. China was required to pay
huge cash indemnities and to permit the stationing of increased numbers of foreign troops on its soil. The leaders of
the Boxer Rebellion were executed, and monuments to for-

eigners who had lost their lives were erected in each of the foreign settlements. The importation of arms and ammunition by China was prohibited for five years. The Chinese government became little more than a debt-collecting agency for foreign powers.

By this time even the dowager empress had been forced to concede that the ancient Chinese Empire was near the end of the road. In the last eight years of her reign she initiated a series of major reforms to salvage what little was left of the Chinese government. Her ministers abolished the official examination system and launched a movement for self-government at the local level. They adopted measures to modernize the army and navy and promised to draft a constitution. These acts, the rulers hoped, would both appease domestic critics and improve China's ability to withstand new foreign assaults. But the reforms were too little and too late. The abolition of the Confucian examination system in 1905 actually speeded up the demise of the Chinese Empire. Henceforth, Western education, not Chinese classical learning, became the key to the public service. This had a most profound effect on the Chinese mind. The ideas and values on which Chinese society and government had traditionally been based were discredited overnight. The monarchy and Empire were doomed. They lasted only another six years.

The shock of the Boxer defeat forced many Chinese, particularly intellectuals, to reevaluate their positions in relation to the West. More and more politically active Chinese came to identify the Manchu dynasty as the source of China's deplorable weakness. Consequently, a whole new generation of students began studying the West in an entirely different light. Nonetheless, like their more radical predecessors, they carefully studied the science and technology of the West while largely ignoring its culture, arts, and literature.

Accompanying this development was a widespread movement for political reform. Young, educated Chinese were attracted to Western ideas of democracy and self-determination—the right of nations to govern themselves. But in China they had little chance to use their skills or develop their political ideas. Government jobs were still in the hands of corrupt Manchu officials, and business was monopolized by foreigners. As a result, many left China to join the communities of overseas Chinese. The most important early figure in this group was Dr. Sun Yat-sen, who founded an organization of Chinese students studying abroad and Chinese intellectuals who stayed in China. These young reformers were Westernized in outlook, but they were also strongly nationalistic. They wanted to get rid of foreign influence in China and begin a program of democratic reforms and economic development. Knowing that nothing would change under the fossilized Manchu government, they worked busily to overthrow it.

The revolution seethed for several years. Suddenly the fortress of Manchu rule crumbled away. The old dowager empress died in 1908. At first, various incompetent officials tried to hold the throne for the heir, the three-year-old Pu-yi. But in 1911 they succumbed to the revolutionary movement. The Republic of China was formally declared. When news of the Nationalist Revolution reached Sun Yat-sen, who was lecturing in the United States, he hurried home to become the first provisional president of the Republic of China.

The Nationalist Revolution ushered in a new era of Chinese history. In the beginning of the nineteenth century the Chinese had turned to the old ways to meet the Western intrusion and had been humiliated. By the mid nineteenth century they had sought to defend themselves by getting Western guns, ships, and arsenals. Very soon they became aware that industry and transport were also essential. Finally, from their contact with the West and the continued desire to rid themselves of the hated foreigners grew feelings of intense nationalism. This nationalism would lead China into radical reform and revolution during the twentieth century.

5

Nationalism and Revolution in China

The Nationalist Revolution of 1911 was like a sledgehammer that demolished a fine old structure. Centuries-old Chinese institutions had been struck down almost overnight. When the Manchu court fell, everyone could see the demoralized and neglected state of affairs the Manchus had left behind in China. China's cities were half owned and run by foreigners, and most of its industry and commerce was in their hands. Chinese peasants lived in a wretchedly impoverished condition. China was a country of chaos and poverty in need of radical change.

The Republic of China, which came into existence in 1912, was dedicated in theory to democracy and modernization. This was the hope at least of younger Chinese intellectuals. During the early years of the twentieth century thousands of young Chinese students attended missionary schools to learn English or went abroad to Japanese and Western universities. The Chinese educated class began to believe that Western learning was valuable and necessary in order to return China to great power status. While abroad, these students studied not only science but, more important, the political economy and political theory of the West. They eagerly imbibed Western democratic ideas. They came to believe that democracy, the political system that made the Western nations strong, was going to save China. They also thought that with the overthrow of the Manchu dynasty, the Westerners would finally accept China as an equal, renounce their concessions, and return the territories they had seized from China. Returning from their studies in Europe and America, these students brought with them the message that under democracy industry would progress, poverty would disappear, and military and national power would revive.

The Republic of China, however, was beset by internal weakness. When established in 1911, it was a parliamentary democracy with a representative assembly, an elected chief of state, and a judiciary. Sun Yat-sen, an ardent nationalist, was the first provisional president of the Republic. However, there was no tradition of self-government at the national level in China. The masses of the people were bewildered and apathetic. Sun described China as "a heap of loose sand." He argued:

> Today we are the poorest and weakest nation in the world, and occupy the lowest position in international affairs. Other men are the carving knife and serving dish; we are the fish and the meat. Our position at this time is most perilous. If we do not earnestly espouse nationalism and weld together our four hundred million people into a strong nation, there is danger of China's being lost and our people being destroyed.

Unfortunately the revolutionary party which Sun headed was a poorly organized group of intellectuals with little popular support. Almost immediately it fell prey to factional strife within its own ranks. It, like China itself, was weak and disunited. Sun Yat-sen also had little military power behind him. As a result, when the Manchus fell and Outer Mongolia and Tibet declared themselves independent, the new Chinese Republic was unable to reconquer these territories. It had its hands full trying to restore the authority of the central government in the provinces of China itself.

It was widely felt that in these circumstances China needed a military strong man to put its house in order. The foreign powers also showed little enthusiasm for Sun Yat-sen and preferred a strong military man who would safeguard their investments. Within one month of being elected provisional president of the Republic of Nanjing, Sun stepped down in order to win the support of Yuan Shikai (Yuan Shih-k'ai), a military leader who had worked for the Manchu dynasty in the last days of the Empire. Yuan, who aspired to be emperor, bypassed the constitution and parliament of the Republic and promulgated a new constitution under which he assumed full governing power. He brought China even further under the control of Western nations by accepting huge foreign loans to pay for the upkeep of his armies.

Yuan Shikai was unable to secure either political unity or the confidence of the Chinese people, and he soon lost the support of his military commanders. When he died suddenly in 1916, China was plunged into several years of local revolt and bitter struggle within the revolutionary movement. Sun Yat-sen's party, now calling itself the Guomindang (Kuomintang) (KMT), set up a government in the southern city of Guangzhou, but North China fell into the hands of local warlords. These power-hungry military governors and ex-bandits carved out their own little empires. They ruthlessly suppressed and exploited the peasants. Throughout the period of warlord rule, things seemed to change only for the worse for the Chinese people. The civil service disintegrated. Civil wars were fought between rival military commanders. Law and order were diminished.

China's military power served only to uphold the rule of corruption and to devastate the provinces. The warlords were out for themselves; they were not concerned with protecting China. They sold more concessions and accepted further foreign loans at high interest rates. The political situation was explosive.

While China was weak and disunited, Japan watched hungrily for every chance to extend its influence. In 1915 Tokyo had pressed twenty-one demands on Yuan Shikai. If accepted, these demands would have placed China under Japanese control. Yuan had successfully eluded most of these demands but had been forced to grant others. For example, China had ceded to Japan a half share in China's most important iron and steel company and had extended leases on railways and ports in the Chinese province of Manchuria, which Japan had seized from Russian ownership in 1905. Japan gained further advantage from China as a result of the First World War. In 1917 the Western Allies had persuaded China to declare war on Germany so that they could attack and seize German possessions in China. However, unknown to China, these possessions had been secretly promised to Japan, which was also on the Allied side. Thousands of Chinese had hoped that President Woodrow Wilson's espousal of national self-determination would somehow protect their country. Thus, when Woodrow Wilson agreed to Tokyo's demand that it retain at least temporary control of former German spheres of influence in China, the Chinese people were outraged. On May 14, 1919, thousands of students organized political demonstrations against foreign intervention and the weak-kneed response of their own government. Shopkeepers, workers, and surprisingly large numbers of peasants came out in support of the students. The corrupt Chinese government of the day was shaken, and a boycott of Japanese goods was initiated.

The May Fourth Movement, as it became known, signaled the birth of modern anti-imperialism in China. Many of the best-educated and politically conscious Chinese had lost faith both in the United States and in the promises of liberal democracy as a tool of reform. It seemed that only a radical and authoritarian political movement might succeed in mobilizing China's masses as a weapon against foreign exploitation. Accompanying this anti-imperialist sentiment was a desire on the part of Chinese intellectuals to be free of the traditional restraints of their society. The old society and China's cultural tradition were questioned and criticized. There were calls for the emancipation of women and changes in the marriage and family system.

In the forefront of the revolutionary enthusiasm of the period were the KMT Nationalists. Active also were a handful of even more radical reformers. They were much impressed by the success of Lenin and the Bolshevik Revolution in Russia and the few Marxist writings they had read. In 1921 these radicals organized the first National Congress of the Chinese Communist Party (CCP) in Shanghai. One of the twelve delegates was Mao Zedong, a young student librarian at Beijing University.

Both the KMT and the CCP felt strongly that China needed a new philosophy which could replace Confucianism. The Republic of China had been a failure, and its attempt at a democracy under Yuan Shikai a farce. Constitutional reform seemed impossible in China. Moreover, the credibility of Western institutions was under attack, particularly after World War I. People of Western nations had just slaughtered one another on an unprecedented scale on the battlefields in Europe and had overturned many of their own institutions in the process. After 1919 both the KMT and the CCP began to look elsewhere for effective programs which would restore China to its former greatness.

Sun Yat-sen's vision of China's future was, nevertheless, a liberal and democratic one. In 1921 he declared the KMT's policy to be the Three People's Principles of nationalism, democracy, and the people's livelihood. The first aim of the KMT was to unite China under a strong national government and to expel foreign influence. The Nationalists demanded the end of unequal treaties, the cancellation of extraterritoriality and foreign control of China's tariffs, and the abolition of leased areas and spheres of influence. Sun Yat-sen eventually wanted democracy for China. But since most Chinese were illiterate and unused to democratic ideas, Sun envisaged a period of tutelage, under KMT leadership, to guide the people toward and educate them for self-government. He also advocated a program to improve the condition of people's lives through land redistribution and industrial modernization. He appealed hopefully to the Western democracies for help with this program but got no response. The Western powers confined themselves to preserving their extraterritorial privileges in the face of the political turmoil in China.

The Chinese Communists shared the KMT attitude of anti-imperialism. Mao Zedong said that by 1919 the main themes in his thoughts were patriotism, resistance to alien rule, self-discipline, social responsibility, and the power of the conscious will to influence events. The Communist program also called for fundamental social and economic changes within China. The Communists embraced Marxism-Leninism and advocated class struggle to liberate China and the Chinese masses from "foreign imperialism and internal exploitation."

Chinese nationalists of varying political beliefs found the doctrine of Marxism-Leninism, particularly its anti-imperialism, appealing. According to Lenin, all the woes of China could be credited to the effects of the expansion of Western capitalism abroad into the developing areas of the world. Many believed this to be not only a convincing explanation of what had happened to China but a doctrine of certain hope for the future. Lenin held that capitalism was dying and that while the downtrodden peoples of the world were threatened by imperialism, in the long run they would make revolution and triumph.

Communist Russia also seemed to the Chinese to be a good ally. Russia was ready to treat China as an equal. Russia renounced its unequal treaties, abolished its concessions, opposed the intervention of other powers in China, and declared that it was ready to help China to become once more truly independent and strong. Even though the Russians neglected to fulfill all their promises, their behavior marked a sharp break from that of other nations toward China. For virtually the first time a Western nation had returned something taken earlier. As a consequence, Russian influence in China in succeeding years would become a major force.

The Chinese Revolution entered a new phase in the early 1920s, when Sun Yat-sen embarked upon a complete reorganization of the KMT. His requests for aid from the West having been ignored, he turned to the Soviet Union for help. Agents of the Russian-dominated Communist International (Comintern) traveled to China and offered material aid and advice in the techniques of revolution. Sun Yat-sen took advantage of this Russian assistance to strengthen his party and army. A young KMT soldier, Chiang Kai-shek, was trained in Russia to head the new Nationalist army school, the Whampoa Military Academy near Guangzhou.

The KMT itself was reorganized on the model of the Soviet Communist Party.

The Comintern agents also encouraged the Chinese Communist Party to support the KMT. Chinese Communists became members of the KMT and joined in 1923 in a United Front against the warlords and the foreign powers. For a short time each party needed the other's skills. The Russians advised the CCP to remain subservient to the KMT in the United Front, to organize urban industrial workers, and to remain unarmed. The KMT, meanwhile, built up its armed strength. The Russian advisers did not expect the KMT to bring communism to China. Rather, they believed the role of the KMT was to mobilize a large cross section of the Chinese people in a popular struggle against the warlords and the foreign powers. According to Moscow, a true proletarian revolution would come later.

Sun Yat-sen died of cancer in 1925. His successor, Chiang Kai-shek, was less idealistic and more conservative than Sun. Despite his training in Moscow, Chiang emerged as a bitter enemy of the Communists. However, the Russians ignored this sign, continued to aid the KMT, and insisted that the CCP do the same.

In 1926 the KMT armies and the CCP political organizers launched the Northern Expedition, a military campaign designed to crush the regional warlords and to unify all of China. The Communists assisted Chiang by spreading through the rural areas to incite the peasants against landlords, by stirring up industrial workers in the foreign-dominated cities, and by gaining control in warlord-ruled areas. These activities soon began to worry some people in the KMT, including Chiang, for the Communists were provoking a real social revolution as they advanced. Foreign governments became alarmed and considered a military intervention to protect their own interests in China. At this point the KMT was forced to decide how far to the left its revolution was going to be.

In 1927 Chiang took control of Nanjing and Shanghai from the warlords and won popular backing. He decided the time was right to get rid of his Comintern advisers and CCP allies. In April 1927 Chiang ordered the KMT to raid the CCP offices in Shanghai with the help of local thugs. Thousands of Communists and their sympathizers were massacred, and the Russian advisers were ejected from China. The few remaining Communists who escaped, including Mao Zedong, either took to the countryside or went into hiding. The United Front between the KMT and the CCP was immediately dissolved. As a result, Soviet policy in China was entirely discredited in the eyes of many Chinese Communists, particularly Mao Zedong.

Chiang Kai-shek's purge of the CCP brought him supremacy in the KMT. At this point he might well have united all of China's revolutionary forces, taken over Western interests in China, and even initiated land reform; however, such actions would have been opposed by the West and might have precipitated a large-scale Western invasion of China. Chiang decided, instead, to consolidate the right wing within the KMT and to expand his army. In order to carry out these plans, he had to increase the financial resources of his party. Therefore, he sought the support of Chinese landlords, merchants, bankers, and industrialists. Chiang also convinced the foreign powers that any violence against foreign interests had been the work of the Communists, who had now been driven underground. He promised to restrain Chinese radicals, to protect foreigners, and to work for the gradual revision of the unequal treaties. Chiang seemed determined to build his own power by gaining the support of powerful groups within China and securing the backing of the industrialized nations.

The KMT army continued its drive northward to unite China. Entering Beijing in 1928, the Northern Expedition against the warlords was formally concluded. Chiang Kaishek became president of the new Republic of China and made Nanjing his capital. Most foreign governments immediately recognized Chiang as the legitimate ruler of China and seemed satisfied that he would be a "reasonable" man to deal with. In the eyes of the West, Chiang had proved himself a responsible nationalist. He was both anti-Communist and willing to ally himself with the rich and powerful in China and abroad. Foreign governments showed their appreciation of him when they agreed to modify certain aspects of the hated unequal treaties. Superficially at least China appeared more unified and stable than it had for almost a half century.

The Communist survivors of the 1927 Shanghai massacre had split into several groups. Some had remained in the cities and loyal to Moscow. Many, however, had fled to the countryside of Central China, where, led by Mao Zedong, they had set out to prove that the Chinese peasants constituted a strong political force. In 1927 Mao had written a controversial report in which he argued that the peasants would be the driving force in China's Revolution. In Mao's words: "In a very short time, in China's central, southern and northern provinces, several hundred million peasants will rise like a mighty storm, like a hurricane, a force so swift and violent that no power, however great, will be able to hold it back." At that time his views were not shared by orthodox Marxists in his own party. The Comintern in Moscow also disagreed with Mao and ordered that the CCP organize in the cities. Ignoring these instructions, later in 1927 Mao organized and led a peasant uprising in his native

Hunan Province. Mao was a little overly optimistic about the strength of a peasant revolt at that time, and the uprising was brutally crushed. From this experience Mao learned that no revolutionary organization could survive in China without a strong army. He was later to write: "Every Communist must grasp the truth. Political power grows out of the barrel of a gun." After 1927 Mao worked hard to develop the techniques needed to achieve a peasant revolution. These were revolutionary warfare coupled with political education and practical work by soldiers and peasants alike. In 1928 Mao joined forces with Zhu De (Chu Teh), another Communist guerrilla, and together they organized the Red Army. From its stronghold in the Jinggang (Chingkang) Mountains the Red Army moved to an area in Jiangxi (Kiangsi) Province. They stayed there for the next five years and tried to establish a model peasant Communist state.

The year 1927, therefore, was very important for the Chinese Revolution. The KMT marched off to the right under Chiang Kai-shek and in the process dropped many of Sun Yat-sen's plans for reforming industry and landownership. The KMT was strong in the cities. By this time, too, it was clear that the KMT was a middle-class party and served the interests of its own middle-class supporters: landlords, businessmen, and financiers. Their wealth and privilege would be threatened by any far-reaching reforms to benefit the masses of peasants and workers. Mao Zedong, on the other hand, believed that the Revolution must grow in the countryside. He advocated an alternative strategy to the one offered by Chiang. Mao initiated a series of land reform experiments which won the support of the peasants. With their support, Mao was able to mobilize an independent peasant force, the Red Army.

During the next twenty years China was plagued by both

foreign invasion and civil war. The KMT and the CCP
fought each other for the control of China's destiny. The
prize for the victor was the Mandate of Heaven and the
right to rule all China.

CHINA AND THE WEST

Shanghai: port of entry for the West

Humiliation at the hands of the West: United States artillerymen attacked Beijing's (Peking's) Tartar Wall during the Boxer Rebellion in 1900. (National Archives)

The wanton destruction of Shanghai during a Japanese air attack in September 1937 helped increase American sympathy for China. (National Archives)

Chiang Kai-shek, Roosevelt, Churchill, and Madame Chiang discussed China's role in World War II at Cairo in 1943. (National Archives)

In former times, the 3,000-mile-long Great Wall protected China's northern borders from invasion by nomadic tribes. Now, with tourism increasing, it is a favorite tourist attraction for Western and Chinese visitors.

Recent political changes have made it possible for the Chinese to buy Western products for the first time in decades. (Neil Taylor)

POLITICS
AND CHANGE

This statue commemorating the Chinese Revolution stands at one end of the Nanking Bridge over the Chang Jiang (Yangtze) River.

Communist soldiers in Shanghai, 1949, celebrate liberation and usher in a new era in Chinese history. (National Archives)

From 1949 until the death of Mao Zedong (Tse-tung), the Chinese people lived under the leadership and ideology of Chairman Mao. His likeness appeared everywhere in statues and posters like this one at the Imperial Palace in Beijing.

Soldiers of the People's Liberation Army raise the famous "Little Red Book," or *Quotations from Mao Zedong,* and chant Maoist slogans at a political rally during the Cultural Revolution.

During the Cultural Revolution, Maoist ideals also dominated Chinese cultural life. Members of a May 7 Cadre School put on a performance to dramatize heroic deeds of China's Red Army.

After the death of Mao Zedong in 1976, Mao's wife, Jiang Qing (Chiang Ching), and the rest of the so-called "Gang of Four" were arrested and tried for a number of political crimes. This poster criticizes them for creating disorder through numerous ideological campaigns. (Neil Taylor)

Political demonstrations such as this one in Beijing denounced the Gang of Four for their high-handed ways during the Cultural Revolution. (Neil Taylor)

THE LONG ROAD TO MODERNIZATION

Peasant farmers still rely on incentives such as selling a portion of their produce at free markets to improve their standard of living. This father and son are on their way to the local market to sell their pig.

To a large extent, industry in China is decentralized, and many goods are produced at the local level. A Chinese factory worker splices rings for metal buckets in a small factory outside Beijing.

Although China hopes to become a modern industrial nation by the year 2000, it is still a developing nation. At a machine tool factory in Henan (Honan) Province, workers operate the blast furnace without benefit of mechanization.

This young woman works in a machine tool factory in Beijing. She is one of an increasing number of Chinese workers who have the opportunity to work with modern precision tools.

Peasants on a commune in north China construct grain storage sheds in traditional style from straw and mud.

The degree of modernization in China varies widely from the countryside to urban areas. Workers at a shipyard in Shanghai construct an ocean-going vessel. (Barbara Lucas)

In Nanjing (Nanking), as in other Chinese cities, the traffic consists mainly of bicycles and pedestrians. Private ownership of automobiles is increasing but is still minimal.

Tricycles are used to haul much of the light freight transported in urban areas.

Although there are some large department stores, most retail trade is still done through small shops or stalls and street markets. At this small shop in Nanjing an abacus is used to calculate the cost of purchases.

A woman sells sewing materials and buttons along the sidewalk in downtown Shanghai.

Advertisements like this for consumer goods have recently begun to reappear in China. They have not been seen for decades. (Neil Taylor)

The Chinese Communist Party still uses its own style of advertising. Political propaganda posters like this one urging workers in a ship-building factory to increase production appear everywhere in China. (Barbara Lucas)

CHINA'S NEXT GENERATION

Peasant children of the Maoist era enthusiastically show the "Little Red Book" to demonstrate their allegiance to Mao Zedong.

Grade school students in Nanjing practice calligraphy, one of the traditional subjects taught.

Politics is also a part of the school curriculum. A group of high school students in Shenyang listen to a speech at a rally on Army Day.

Students at a Nanjing middle school cooperate in the growing of food in their garden at school.

OPPOSITE: Young people are often required to do hard physical labor. A peasant girl wheels her cart down a country road.

Physical exercise is also a part of most school curriculums. Middle school students at August First People's Commune outside Shenyang jump rope.

Young boys practice traditional martial arts at a Children's Palace in Shanghai.

These girls have found a cool corner at the Summer Palace for a game of cards—a favorite pastime for many young people in China.

Ice cream is a treat for Chinese of all ages. Teenagers buy popsicles from a vendor in a public park.

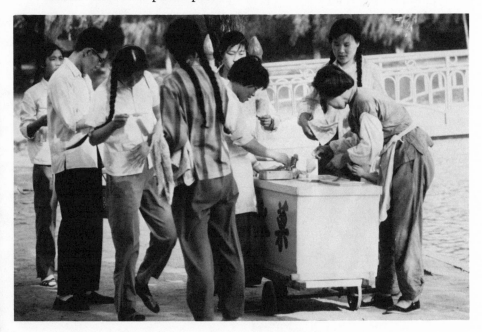

Young people under the
age of sixteen years
constitute over 40
percent of the population
in China. The attitudes
and values of the young,
therefore, are crucial to
China's future.

6

Foreign Invasion
and Civil War in China

After 1927, when the KMT gained control of the cities, there was for the first time since the death of Yuan Shikai a government in China that could be regarded seriously. However, although Chiang had gained control of the cities and had won foreign recognition for his regime, the KMT never really controlled the countryside. It exercised firm control in only two provinces and partial control in eight others. In most of the other eighteen provinces, Chiang allowed his military generals and the warlords to retain power on condition that they acknowledge the supremacy of the central government. Consequently, KMT power never penetrated to the local level. The landlords and gentry continued to dominate rural life.

The Nationalist government, nevertheless, did attempt to start China on the road to modernization and did bring about limited progress. Chiang's government encouraged achievements in the fields of communication and industry and initiated some reforms in education. For example, the KMT introduced the New Life Movement, which attempted to teach people the value of honesty and devotion to the public welfare. The Nationalist government even proclaimed a complete set of modern laws. In foreign policy the KMT hoped gradually to terminate the unequal treaties, extraterritoriality, and foreign leaseholds. Social reform also had some significance. The status of women was improved in Nationalist China. Foot-binding was outlawed, and for the first time in Chinese history some women gained access to education.

The gap between paper reform and political reality was, however, considerable. Even at the height of KMT power in the mid-1930s, foreign interests still controlled 95 percent of China's iron; three-quarters of its coal; half its textile production; most of its shipping; the bulk of public utilities; and much of its banking, insurance, and trade. Half the industrial workers in Shanghai were employed by foreign firms. Nonetheless, under Chiang the privileges of foreigners in China were curtailed somewhat. For instance, China's right to control its own tariffs was restored in 1928. But the Western powers were to cling to their right of extraterritoriality until 1943. Western imperialism in China was not finally defeated until the Communists came to power in 1949.

Chiang Kai-shek's political model for the KMT came not from the democratic West, but from China's Confucian past. Chiang was a traditionalist. Once he assumed complete power in 1927, he looked for inspiration more and more to the example of imperial China. Chiang ceased to consider the KMT a spearhead of revolution and came to regard the party as an instrument for restoring order. In the view of the KMT leaders, Confucianism was the cheapest and most effective means ever devised for this purpose. According to Chiang, the country could be saved only if it recovered its "true national spirit" and remembered that "for several thousand years our country has considered loyalty and filial piety as the basis of the state."

Chiang repeatedly tried to put these principles of discipline and loyalty into effect. In 1928 he urged KMT army officers and teachers to revive Confucian classics and ideology. In 1931 he declared Confucius's birthday a national holiday. In the countryside Chiang tried to build up the position of the gentry. Old privileges were restored, and new ones added, in the hope that the gentry might once again play their traditional role of maintaining local order. Unfortunately Chiang failed to appreciate the fact that the restoration of the old order had already been tried under more hopeful circumstances and found wanting.

Chiang never seriously intended to create a democratic system in China. The Nationalist government steadily evolved toward a dictatorship. Under KMT rule, there was no protection of human rights and no government by majority decision. Instead, Chiang and a small clique of wealthy men remained in complete control of all political activities by censoring the press and maintaining a strong secret police. This force, headed by General Dai Li (Tai Li), helped to stifle any criticism of the Nationalist government. Chiang consolidated all power and decision making in his own hands. Eventually he himself held more than eighty government posts simultaneously.

The KMT had a number of fatal flaws, but the fundamental weakness was its failure to do anything for the peasants. Although China remained an overwhelmingly agricultural country, social improvements initiated by the KMT mainly benefited the minority of the Chinese people who lived in the cities. The 90 percent of the population who lived in China's vast countryside remained largely untouched by the new laws. No efforts at real land reform were undertaken. Some laws to reduce rents and taxes were passed, but they were routinely ignored by provincial officials and landlords. Chiang had no desire to challenge local vested interests. He feared that, once launched, a land reform program might gain too much momentum and turn against the KMT. Hence, he became increasingly tied to the ultraconservative landlords. He was insensitive to the plight of Chinese peasants and their demands for basic social justice.

During the 1920s and 1930s the economic condition of the peasants steadily worsened in most parts of the countryside. In order to meet the rising cost of arms for the warlords and the KMT army and in order to pay off China's huge foreign loans, Chiang's government levied higher and higher taxes on the peasants. In some provinces warlords exacted taxes as much as fifty years in advance. Many peasants had to mortgage or sell their lands to pay taxes, and most of the land that could be cultivated was sold to the landlords. Peasants were forced to live on what had been their own land as tenants who were almost always in debt to their landlords. In many places the landlords, their relatives, and their friends were also the tax collectors, the moneylenders, the local officials, and the store owners who controlled the prices of the goods bought and sold in the area.

When famine occurred, the landless peasants often were unable to meet the crisis. Since there was no organized government relief, millions of peasants died of starvation. The American journalist Edgar Snow painted a terrible picture of conditions during the great famine of 1928 to 1930 in China's Northwest. He wrote of men whose flesh hung from them in folds; children with misshapen bodies, twig-like arms, and bloated stomachs; women with protruding buttocks and breasts hanging like empty sacks. Snow also described how in the towns there were still rich men with hoards of grain to sell at inflated prices, while in the cities of Beijing and Tianjin lay thousands of tons of wheat and millet which were not shipped to the starving because the warlords who controlled the railroad rolling stock were afraid to risk the possibility that rival warlords might seize the trains.

During that famine 5 million people died, and thousands of acres of land were bought by speculators for ridiculously low prices. Four hundred thousand women and children were sold into slavery. Snow described how some people even sold their clothes and wandered around the countryside naked. Peasants ate tree bark, roots, straw, leaves, and earth to relieve their hunger.

No patriotic Chinese could long remain insensitive to the plight of the peasants during such dreadful times. Chiang Kai-shek's failure to assist the poor was his greatest failing. While millions of peasants starved, Nationalist officials and generals hoarded vast storehouses of grain to sell at high prices on the black market.

From their stronghold in the Jinggang Mountains Mao and his Red Army had moved in 1928 to an area in Jiangxi Province in Central China, where they stayed for the next several years and tried to establish a model Communist state. Mao Zedong believed that the peasants were the most important part of the Revolution and that winning their support should be the key part of Chinese Communist strategy. In the countryside the Communists began a series of experiments in land reform. Their proclamation of radical land reform aroused age-old peasant grievances against landlords. A thirst for vengeance poured forth in a wave of violence. The peasants killed many landlords and seized their lands. Where the Communists took control, the debts of peasants were canceled, and peasant associations were set up to run the areas with the help of the CCP and the Red Army. In his writings, even Mao admitted that the treatment of landlords in Jiangxi was too heavy-handed. In particular, the rights of the "middle peasants" who owned land and were not so desperately poor were violated. However, this was a learning period for the CCP. By degrees, the Communists mastered the method of mobilizing widespread support. Consequently, despite the violent nature of the land reform program at this early stage, they won many peasants over to their side. The Communists also initiated numerous propaganda programs designed to encourage the peasants to tie their futures to their cause. These policies and programs were successful in recruiting thousands of peasant volunteers for the Red Army.

At this time the Communists were under constant attack from the KMT; as a result, they learned and applied revolutionary guerrilla warfare. A key element of Red Army strategy was development of close ties with the peasants. In many respects, the Red Army was a new kind of military unit in China. Unlike the warlord and KMT armies, the soldiers did not extort their living from the peasants, eating their grain and raping their women. They were disciplined and helped the peasants in their work whenever they could. They lived by a strict eight-point code of behavior:

1. Speak politely.
2. Pay fairly for what you buy.
3. Return everything you borrow.
4. Pay for anything you damage.
5. Don't hit or swear at people.
6. Don't damage crops.
7. Don't take liberties with women.
8. Don't ill-treat prisoners.

Chiang Kai-shek was determined to crush the Red Army before it grew too strong. Between 1931 and 1934 the Nationalist army launched five massive bandit extermination campaigns against the Communists in Jiangxi. Finally, in 1934, the KMT army, with its vastly superior arms, was on the verge of overrunning the Communist base. Mao and 100,000 troops broke out of the encirclement and began what became known as the Long March. Mao's forces had

no vehicles and few horses, so they walked—a year-long re-
treat covering more than 6,000 miles. Only about 20,000 of
the original force reached the final destination at Yan'an
(Yenan) in mountainous Shaanxi (Shensi) Province of China's remote Northwest. The Long March was one of the
great feats of military history and is celebrated in poems
and operas throughout China today.

Those who survived this ordeal were even more determined to launch a revolution against the KMT. The soldiers
of the Red Army who reached Yan'an provided an extremely dedicated and tough core for future Communist expansion. In addition, the Chinese Communist Party had
become fully and fiercely independent, with only nominal
ties to Moscow. For the next nine years the North remained
the center of Red Army activities. There the Communists
lived in caves they dug in sandy hills. From this base they
recruited and trained a vast peasant army. They developed
a Communist state within China, complete with government, schools, and even a university. Communist Party officials, called cadres, particularly Mao Zedong, gave
frequent lectures to thousands of Red Army recruits at the
famous "cave university" in Yan'an. Mao's lectures and es-
says from the Yan'an period formed the basic philosophy of
the Chinese Communist Revolution.

While the struggle between KMT and CCP forces unfold-
ed, Nationalist China faced an even graver threat from an
aggressive Japan. The worldwide Great Depression, which
had begun in America in 1929, had threatened Japan's dynamic economy and trading position. As international trade
plummeted and credit shriveled, Japanese exports were
frozen out of Western markets. China, which had been a
major source of raw materials and an important export market for Japan, became increasingly significant to Tokyo.
Japanese militants feared that a resurgent China under

Chiang Kai-shek's leadership might threaten Japan's economic position still more, so they decided to protect themselves by expanding Japanese interests in China. In 1931 Japanese forces struck quickly. They met little resistance and occupied Manchuria in Northeast China. There they set up a puppet state called Manchukuo. Chiang Kai-shek appealed to the League of Nations for help, but the League failed to agree on how to stop the Japanese aggression. Japan's control gradually spread into Northern China and Inner Mongolia and ultimately threatened the heartland of China.

Despite these mounting external threats to China's security, Chiang concentrated nearly all his attention and strength against his domestic rivals, the Communists. Late in 1936 he journeyed to the city of Xi'an (Sian) near Yan'an to prod his reluctant military commanders to intensify the campaign against the Communists. At Xi'an, Chiang was kidnapped by his own generals. They hoped to persuade him that it was foolish to waste strength fighting Communists while the invading Japanese were the real enemy of Nationalists and Communists alike. After a week of arguments Chiang was released. The KMT and the Communists agreed to a second united front. The Red Army officially became the Eighth Route Army under Chiang's command, but cooperation between KMT and CCP forces existed in name only. Both Chiang and Mao knew that their truce was only temporary and that, once Japan was defeated, they would return to their life-and-death struggle for the control of China.

In July 1937 the Japanese war machine began its all-out attack on China, thus beginning World War II in Asia in earnest. These invaders were greatly superior in military organization and arms. In response, China could fight only a war of resistance. At first, the KMT army made valiant stands;

nonetheless, by 1939 Japan had occupied the eastern third of China. Rather than sacrifice his strength in what appeared to be a futile campaign, Chiang settled for a strategy of "trading space to buy time." The KMT retreated into the interior of the country to Chongqing (Chungking) and tried to exhaust the enemy by protracted opposition. For the remainder of World War II Chiang made no attempt to launch a major counteroffensive. He preferred to adopt a passive defense, waiting until either Japan overextended itself or the United States entered the war. Consequently, after 1938 the only significant battles of KMT troops were occasional attacks on their Communist allies in the Northwest.

In the United States the massive and brutal Japanese attack on China had a profound effect upon American public opinion. The terror bombing of defenseless Chinese cities and the deliberate pillage by invading Japanese troops seemed barbaric. In the American press Japanese soldiers were portrayed as bloodthirsty and subhuman. Americans reacted with horror and a general outpouring of sympathy for the Chinese people. Because China continued to resist Japan against heavy odds, Chiang Kai-shek assumed heroic proportions in the American mind. Chiang was widely hailed as a hero, savior, and "indispensable leader." *Time* magazine designated Generalissimo and Madame Chiang Kai-shek "Man and Wife of the Year" in 1938 and asserted that Chiang "had remade China" and that "after centuries, the Chinese people had at last found a leader." Much was also made of the fact that Chiang was a Christian; Western missionaries praised him effusively despite his repressive regime.

In spite of tremendous sympathy for China in its long struggle against Japan, neither American leaders nor the American public believed that the United States should rush to the defense of Chiang. Isolationist sentiment was strong throughout American society in the late 1930s. Moreover, Asia seemed a world away at a time when war in Europe and resistance to Nazi Germany preoccupied American concerns. Because China was not part of the European conflict, the United States did not extend aid to Chiang.

After 1937 Chiang did, however, receive substantial military help from the Soviet Union. Joseph Stalin, the undisputed Soviet dictator, feared Japanese power in the Far East and the threat it posed to Russian interests there. In addition, the Soviets were apprehensive about the threat Japan might pose to eastern Russia. Believing that the best way to deter Japanese expansionism was to keep Tokyo's armies tied down in China, Stalin offered massive aid to the KMT. By 1941 Soviet aid amounted to $250 million in military loans, 885 planes, provisions for twenty-four Chinese divisions, 400 Soviet advisers, and several hundred Soviet pilots. Virtually all this aid went to the KMT; as a result, on a number of occasions Soviet supplies were used by Chiang against Communist forces. This aid to Chiang strained Soviet relations with Mao and the Chinese Communists. However, at the time Stalin had more faith in the existing Nationalist regime than in a small, unproved Chinese Communist movement in Yan'an which was not under his personal control.

When Japan attacked Pearl Harbor in December 1941, China's cause immediately became of great interest to the United States and the Allies. Henceforth, China became one of the Big Five alliance against the Axis powers of Germany and Japan. Chiang Kai-shek privately welcomed the news of the Pearl Harbor attack because he knew the U.S. entry into the Pacific war would open the tap of American aid which he had been eagerly awaiting. During the next few years the United States gave millions of dollars of aid in materials and weapons to the KMT.

No ally could have been more appealing to Americans than China. American missionaries and businessmen had been in China since the nineteenth century, and there was widespread sympathy for the "underdog" Chinese. Americans felt that there was a "special relationship" between the United States and China and that America should act as protector or "big brother." Hence, when war ended American isolationism, nothing seemed more fitting than an American-Chinese alliance. The United States was fighting for China's territorial integrity. And according to KMT propaganda, the Chinese were showing their gratitude by engaging huge Japanese armies on the mainland and thus saving American lives in the Pacific. Moreover, the United States placed great hope in the future role China would play in Asia. In the American view, a stable, moderate, and reform-minded China could be the linchpin for the security of all Asia after the war. Furthermore, a pro-American China would be useful as a buffer against possible Soviet expansion in Northeast Asia.

It soon became apparent, however, that Chiang Kai-shek and President Franklin Roosevelt viewed the war differently. Americans saw the war as a two-sided struggle, the Allies versus the Axis. Chiang's triangular view saw the antagonists as the Nationalist government, the Japanese, and the Chinese Communists. The KMT army had done almost no fighting since 1938, and Chiang could see little reason to engage the Japanese after the Americans entered the war in 1941. He was counting on the United States to defeat Japan while he hoarded the currency, gold, and weapons delivered to him. Chiang was saving his strength for his internal enemies, the Communists. "The Japanese are only a disease of the skin, but communism is a disease of the heart," he said.

Most foreign observers failed to realize the momentous changes occurring in China. Most Americans were divorced from the reality of the situation in China and had only the dimmest comprehension of Chinese conditions. Missionaries, government officials, businessmen, and American military personnel were absorbed in the pressing daily tasks of cooperating with their new ally. Although they knew of Chiang's reluctance to fight and of the tyranny and corruption of his government, they also had a long-standing emotional and financial commitment to the KMT and a strong dislike of communism. Few were willing to push Chiang Kai-shek too hard to undertake reforms for fear that such action would hasten the destruction of the KMT.

A handful of journalists and American Foreign Service officers made genuine efforts to find out what was really happening and to report what they found back to the United States. Tragically KMT censorship blocked most of the news stories from reaching America. For example, KMT censorship prevented the American journalist Theodore White from filing this eyewitness report of the 1942–1943 famine in Henan (Honan) Province:

> The peasants as we saw them were dying. They were dying on the roads, in the mountains, by the railway stations, in their mud huts, in the fields. And as they died, the government continued to wring from them the last possible ounce of tax. . . . The government in county after county was demanding of the peasant more . . . grain than he had raised. . . . No excuses were allowed; peasants who were eating elm bark and dried leaves had to haul their last sack of grain to the tax collector's office.

Peasants who were so weak they could barely walk had to collect fodder for the army's horses. . . . One of the most macabre touches of all of this was the flurry of land speculation. Merchants . . . small government officials, army officials and rich land owners who still had food were engaged in purchasing the peasant's ancestral areas at criminally low figures . . . we knew that there was a fury, as cold and as relentless as death itself, in the bosom of the peasants of Honan, that their loyalty had been hollowed to nothingness by the extortion of their government.

Criticisms of Chiang Kai-shek and the Nationalist government were routinely ignored in Washington. American reports of conditions in China under KMT rule made horrifying reading. Nonetheless, President Roosevelt and his close advisers had committed the United States to cooperation with the KMT, and they were unable or unwilling to alter their course.

7

The Collapse of Chiang Kai-shek

The entire KMT government structure rested on bribery and the loyalty of interest groups. Chiang was like a juggler, playing army generals, warlords, scholars, and businessmen against one another in a pattern of threats and payoffs that kept his system going. Corruption and inefficiency were widespread, and the economy was bankrupt. Inflation was so bad that money ceased to have any real value. Suitcases crammed with bank notes were used to pay for the most basic items. Because inflation particularly affected the middle classes, which had previously backed Chiang, they lost confidence in the Nationalists' ability to govern.

Under such economic conditions, the only possible way to maintain KMT armies in the field was by allowing generals to conscript men in any way they could and to supply the troops by bleeding the peasants. In a report prepared in 1945 American military officials described the formation of a typical KMT unit:

> Conscription: Conscription comes to the Chinese peasant like famine or flood, only more regularly—every year twice— and claims more victims. Famine, flood, and drought compare with conscription like chicken pox with plague.
>
> The virus is spread over the Chinese countryside. . . . There is first the press gang. For example, you are working in the field looking after your rice. . . . [There comes] a number of men

who tie your hands behind your back and take you with them. . . . Hoe and plow rust in the field, the wife runs to the magistrate to cry and beg for her husband, the children starve.

In addition, the KMT army was crippled from within by weak leadership, low morale, and corruption. Generals pocketed funds intended for payment of their troops. Chinese soldiers were treated as cannon fodder. According to the 1945 American military report:

> If somebody dies, his body is left behind. His name on the list is carried along. As long as his death is not reported, he continues to be a source of income, increased by the fact that he has ceased to consume. His rice and his pay become a long-lasting token of memory in the pocket of his commanding officer. His family will have to forget him.

In contrast with the KMT, the Communists spent the war years struggling against Japan and building a mass peasant army. Although they fought few large-scale battles with the Japanese, the Communists harassed Japanese supply lines and communications with thousands of guerrilla actions. In the KMT army, equipment rusted from disuse and men died of starvation before they saw combat. The Red Army, on the other hand, used the experience of fighting the Japanese to improve morale, discipline, and organization. They won widespread support by offering national resistance to the Japanese occupation forces. At the same time the Communists built up a stable organization within the villages through a moderate land reform program. Instead of outright confiscation of land and the murder of landlords, as had been the practice in Jiangxi, the Communists persuaded the landlords to reduce their land rent. Landlords were allowed to retain most of their property as long as they went along with party policy.

These tactics yielded high returns in peasant support for the Communists. The peasants became convinced of two things: Not only were the Communists dedicated to the patriotic struggle against Japan, but the peasants themselves had a direct stake in the survival and victory of the CCP. The Communist Party became their representative. It voiced their demands for social and economic justice against the landlord class. Moreover, peasants were treated as valuable human beings by the Communists and weren't swindled, beaten, and kicked about, as they were by the KMT forces. The peasants responded by flocking to join the Red Army. In 1937 the Communists could claim control of only a few thousand square miles, a million people, and an army of 80,000. Eight years later, when Japan surrendered, the Communists commanded a million troops, occupied one-quarter of China, and governed 100 million people. During the Second World War the Communists had begun to win China and the KMT to lose it.

At the same time Americans became increasingly irritated when they realized that the money and supplies they were sending to help the Chinese war effort were producing so little result. By 1942 the KMT capital at Chongqing was almost completely isolated from the outside world. Then, when the Japanese took Burma, they closed the Burma Road and thus cut off China's outside source of supply. China continued to be supplied only via the "Hump," a hazardous airlift over the Himalayas from North India. The amount of equipment brought into China via this route was hardly enough to fill even the most basic needs.

In the spring of 1942 Washington sent General Joseph "Vinegar Joe" Stilwell to China to open up the Burma Road and to keep the KMT army fighting so that the Japanese could not divert any troops from China to the Pacific battleground. Stilwell was an old China hand. He knew China well, spoke Chinese, and had a deep respect and love for the Chinese people. He was also a blunt, straight-talking military man known for his salty remarks and peppery personality. The difficulty was that Stilwell had to work through the generally incompetent and corrupt KMT military command. Thus, when he wanted to train a division of Chinese troops to be sent on a campaign to open up the Burma Road, Chiang balked at the plan. He was reluctant to commit his troops to battle against the Japanese because he was saving them to use against the Communists.

Exasperated at Chiang's unwillingness to fight, Stilwell advised President Roosevelt to get tough with Chiang and demand basic reforms in the KMT government in return for further shipments of American aid. At the same time, he told Chiang to "patch things up with Mao Zedong" and fight alongside him against the Japanese in a new coalition government. Chiang did everything possible to prevent these reforms and shifts in KMT policy. But even if he had wanted to reform the country at that late date, Chiang could not choose to remove his friends from power or relinquish his own job. Nor did he want to strengthen the Communists by allowing them into the government. It was clear by 1942 that the KMT-CCP United Front was dissolving. The Nationalists had already clashed with the Communists in one major battle in 1941; by 1942 open conflict between Chiang and Mao had resumed.

Stilwell concluded that the military crisis in China was a result of the breakdown of principle, policy, and administration in the KMT government. Inflation, corruption, and starvation were endemic, and the political situation was further aggravated by the deadlock between the KMT and the Communists. According to Stilwell, the architect of the "whole manure pile" was Chiang Kai-shek. The following extracts from the papers of General Stilwell reflect his views of conditions in China:

> Chiang Kai-shek is confronted with an idea, and that defeats him. He is bewildered by the spread of Communist influence. He can't see that the mass of Chinese people welcome the Reds as being the only visible hope of relief from crushing taxation, the abuses of the Army and [the terror of] Tai Li's Gestapo. Under Chiang Kai-shek they now begin to see what they may expect. Greed, corruption, favoritism, more taxes, a ruined currency, terrible waste of life, callous disregard of all the rights of men.
>
> I judge Kuomintang and the Communist Party by what I saw:
>
> [KMT] corruption, neglect, chaos, economy, taxes, words and deeds. Hoarding, black market, trading with the enemy.
>
> Communist program . . . reduce taxes, rents, interest. Raise production and standard of living. Participate in government. Practice what they preach.
>
> The cure for China's trouble is the elimination of Chiang Kai-shek. The only thing that keeps this country split is his fear of losing control. He hates the Reds and will not take any chances on giving them a toehold in the government.

As a result of these critical reports from Stilwell and growing American dissatisfaction with Chiang Kai-shek, President Roosevelt came to the opinion that the only hope for unifying China was to revitalize the United Front between the KMT and the CCP. In 1944 an American military group, the Dixie Mission, visited the Communist base in Yan'an. It reported that American aid might be better used if it were sent directly to the Communists. A number of leading American Foreign Service officers also strongly urged a shift in U.S. China policy. Tang Tsou describes the attitude of these younger American diplomats in his book *America's Failure in China*. John Service reported: "Any new Chinese government under any other than the present reactionary control will be more cooperative with the United States and better able to mobilize the country." John Paton Davies wrote:

> We must be realistic. We must not indefinitely underwrite a politically bankrupt regime. We must make a determined effort to capture politically the Chinese Communists rather than allow them to go by default wholly to the Russians. Furthermore, we must fully understand that by reason of our recognition of the Chiang Kai-shek government as now constituted we are committed to a steadily decaying regime and severely restricted in working out military and political cooperation with the Chinese Communists. . . . Power in China is on the verge of shifting from Chiang to the Communists.

At the time of the Dixie Mission the Chinese Communists were excited by the possibility of American political recognition and military aid. They were only too aware that Chiang Kai-shek had surrounded the Yan'an base area with one of his crack divisions in order to prevent any outside supplies from reaching the Communists. However, with U.S. support, Mao Zedong hoped to break through Chiang's military blockade. Mao assured the visiting Americans that they had nothing to fear from the Communists. "Even the most conservative American businessman can find nothing in our program" to object to, he claimed. The Communists did not deny their commitment to a Chinese revolution, but they also constantly asserted their belief that they and Washington had certain parallel interests in China. The American diplomat John Service recalled that Mao said:

America does not need to fear we will not cooperate. We must cooperate and we must have American help. This is why it is important to us Communists to know what you Americans are thinking and planning. We cannot risk crossing you—cannot risk conflict with you.

This cooperation never came to pass. Chiang Kai-shek feared cutbacks in U.S. aid and vigorously protested any changes in American policy toward the Communists. Fortunately for Chiang he had powerful American connections. Henry Luce, publisher of *Time* and *Life,* idolized the Nationalists and promoted their interests in his influential magazines. Madame Chiang Kai-shek made several successful tours of the United States to convince Americans of the unbreakable bond of unity between the United States and China and of the KMT's dynamic fighting spirit. Chiang cooperated with those Americans who were jealous of or disagreed with critical Americans such as Stilwell and who hoped to boost their own careers through working with the KMT. This old Chinese strategy of playing the barbarians off against each other worked. In October 1944 Chiang convinced Roosevelt to order General Stilwell to come home. Stilwell's successor was General Albert Wedemeyer. American aid continued to flow to the Nationalists in Chongqing rather than to the Chinese Communists in Yan'an.

Roosevelt also soon sent Patrick J. Hurley, a former Republican secretary of war and Washington gadfly, to China as his special representative to Chiang Kai-shek. Hurley's mission was to try to arrange a coalition government between the KMT and the CCP that would unify China. In November 1944 he flew to Yan'an to negotiate with the Communists. As he stepped off the plane to be met by Zhou Enlai and other Communist leaders, Hurley shocked everyone by emitting an Indian war whoop and slapping people on the back in greeting. Privately he referred to the Communist leaders as "Mouse Dung" and "Joe N. Lie." His antics failed to impress the Communists, however, and he was not able to pressure them into a minor role in a KMT-dominated government. Hurley and Chiang Kai-shek demanded that the Communists dissolve the Red Army and accept some token political appointments to the KMT government. Naturally, as negotiator for the Communists, Zhou Enlai rejected this offer on the ground that it would be mass suicide for the Communists. The Communists insisted that in any coalition they share real power and maintain their separate army.

Disappointed with American policy, the CCP made a final effort to change Roosevelt's mind about China. In January 1945 Mao and Zhou offered to travel to Washington to meet the President and make a personal appeal for American support. Hurley learned of this offer and warned Roosevelt against dealing with the CCP. He claimed that the Communists had refused to reach a fair settlement with the KMT because disloyal Americans had joined them in a conspiracy against Chiang Kai-shek. Roosevelt backed his ambassador and authorized the removal from China of any American whom Hurley considered "disloyal." During the next several months Hurley made members of his staff swear their loyalty to his own views and even threatened to shoot one young diplomat who had the gall to criticize Chiang and the KMT.

In August 1945 the United States dropped two atomic bombs on Japan. Tokyo surrendered within days. Both the KMT and the Communists raced to seize control of the territory and weapons held by the Japanese in China. Mao Zedong had urged the United States to take a neutral position between the KMT and the CCP. However, immediately

upon Japan's surrender President Harry Truman ordered
all Japanese forces in China to surrender their positions and
arms to Chiang Kai-shek or his representatives. More than
50,000 American marines were rushed from the Pacific to
be redeployed along vital rail lines, ports, and airfields in
North China. The United States also airlifted half a million
KMT troops from South China to Northeast China in order
to prevent the Communists from sweeping in from the
countryside to gain control of the cities. Although Soviet armies had occupied Manchuria in the final days of the war,
the Russians were mainly concerned with their own interests in China and were indifferent to the fate of the Chinese
Communists. After presenting the Red Army with limited
stockpiles of captured Japanese weapons, the Russians
handed Manchuria over to the KMT as the legal government of China. They also took advantage of their occupation of Manchuria to strip it of more than $2 billion worth
of factory machinery and railroad supplies, which they took
home as "war booty." Then they waited for the outcome of
the Chinese civil war without giving further assistance to
the Chinese Communists.

Not particularly optimistic that Chiang Kai-shek could
win a war with the Communists, the United States sought
a coalition government which would allow him to retain
some, if not all, of his power. In late 1945 President Truman
dispatched General George Marshall to China with instructions to act as mediator between the two sides. Marshall's
initial discussions with the two groups seemed hopeful, and
he was able to arrange a cease-fire in January 1946. However, the terms of the agreement were constantly violated.
Neither Chiang nor Mao could agree to concessions which
might impede ultimate victory. Consequently, the talks
broke down, civil war resumed, and Marshall headed back
to the United States in early 1947 to become secretary of

state. The last phase of the long struggle for power in China had begun in earnest.

Having failed to achieve a diplomatic solution in 1946, the United States now poured several billion dollars of money and weapons into China during 1947 and 1948. At the outset of the civil war the KMT army was much stronger than the Communist Red Army. Chiang's military strategy concentrated on holding the cities of the North and Manchuria, while trying at the same time to meet the Communists head-on in major battles. For their part, the Red Army chose to engage the KMT forces in small combat operations because the Communists knew their strength lay in guerrilla warfare and popular support. By relying on a static and essentially defensive strategy, the Nationalists left themselves open to Communist encirclement and harassment. The Communists took advantage of their own mobility to cut Chiang's forces off from their sources of supply. They used time and guerrilla tactics to wear down the fighting abilities and morale of their opponents.

No amount of American aid could stop the Nationalist rot. By this time U.S. money merely gave the KMT added opportunities for corruption. Nationalist soldiers were seldom paid and were usually abused by their officers. Most American aid was diverted to the black market by corrupt KMT officials or was hoarded in the treasury or in government hideaways. Soaring inflation and food shortages made daily life impossible for everyone. The few remaining supporters of the KMT finally backed away in disgust at this final display of corruption and mismanagement.

In 1948 the Communists launched the final offensive. After scoring major victories in Manchuria, Mao's forces pushed steadily and quickly through the rest of China, meeting very little resistance along the way. Morale and politics, not military tactics, determined the outcome of the civil war. In their twenty-year struggle the Communists had won over the masses, and now even the middle classes were willing to give them a chance. The KMT army had been destroyed from within by weak leadership and sagging morale. Entire KMT divisions surrendered their American-made weapons without even firing a shot. The Communists swept southward, joking about their "Supply Sergeant Chiang." Unsupported by soldiers at the front or by civilians in the cities, the Nationalist cause collapsed, and the KMT was routed.

By late 1948 the United States had cut off all aid to Chiang Kai-shek. Most responsible American political leaders, however great their dislike of Chinese communism, simply did not believe that the United States could "save" the KMT. Under fierce attack by a number of disappointed congressmen, the State Department issued a White Paper in August 1949 absolving the United States of responsibility for the Chinese government's fall. Secretary of State Dean Acheson summed up the government's position:

> The . . . inescapable fact is that the ominous result of the civil war in China was beyond the control of the government of the United States. Nothing that this country did or could have done within the reasonable limits of its capabilities could have changed that result.
>
> . . . It was the product of internal Chinese forces, forces which this country tried to influence but could not.

In May 1949 the Communists crossed the Chang Jiang and took Shanghai. In September the Chiangs, the Nationalist government, hundreds of millions of hoarded dollars, and about half a million KMT troops fled to Taiwan, an island 100 miles off the south coast of China. On October 1, 1949, in Beijing, Mao Zedong proclaimed the People's Republic of China and declared that "the Chinese people have stood up."

The new Communist rulers led a strong national government that had come to power without outside help. They had a record of patriotic resistance to foreign imperialists and had defeated the American-backed KMT. They offered the hope of a strong and independent China in years to come. The Mandate of Heaven, that right to rule which the Chinese recognized as conferring legitimacy on a government, had passed to the victorious Chinese Communists and Mao Zedong.

Mao Zedong
and the Chinese Way

When Mao Zedong and the Chinese Communists took control of China in 1949, they turned their attention to restoring order to their war-torn country. A revolution had been going on in China for more than a century and had gone through many stages. Upon assuming power, the Communists carried the revolution to its irrevocable conclusion by sweeping away the entire institutional structure of the old system and, with it, those classes that had maintained that system—officials, gentry, landlords, and foreigners.

Mao had expounded his ideas on the new order in China in a pamphlet entitled *On the People's Democratic Dictatorship.* He had said, "You are quite right, my dear sirs; that is just what we are—a democracy for the people and a dictatorship for the reactionaries." He defined the people as the working class, the peasantry, the urban bourgeoisie, and those merchants and industrialists who worked with the Communists. Only the people should form the state, choose the government, enjoy freedom of speech and assembly and the right to vote. The reactionaries, including landlords, rich peasants, capitalists, and KMT sympathizers, were "class enemies" and should be reformed, suppressed, or executed. Mao had written elsewhere: "A revolution is not a dinner party, or writing an essay, or painting a picture, or doing embroidery; it cannot be so re-

118

fined, so leisurely and gentle, so temperate, kind, courte-
ous, restrained or magnanimous. A revolution is an
insurrection, an act of violence by which one class over-
throws another."

When the Communists came to power, they remained
true to Mao's principles. The war-weary people they led
were eager to accept almost any authority that could restore order. After driving Chiang Kai-shek out of China in
1949, Mao turned his attention immediately toward con-
trolling hyperinflation. He quickly and effectively stabi-
lized prices. He also introduced rationing and a policy of
building grain reserves for keeping people fed when har-
vests failed. The CCP had come to power by organizing and
mobilizing the rural poor. Under Mao, the party continued
to promote rural interests. Land reform doubled the average holding of the poorest half of China's peasant farmers.
Credit systems sprang up so that now farmers could borrow
money instead of either selling their land or starving during
bad years. Paid work outside the home opened up new opportunities for women. Thus, the standard of living for the
average peasant rose considerably in Maoist China. At the
same time "reactionaries," those people whom the Communists considered unsuitable for integration into the new
order, were being harshly dealt with in a series of political
campaigns. The land reform movement of 1950 to 1952
took land away from the landlords and redistributed it to
poor and middle-level peasants. The Communists encouraged the peasants "to speak their bitterness" against years
of oppression at the hands of landlords. As a result, hundreds of thousands of "reactionary" landlords were accused
of various crimes before large assemblies, were condemned
by the "masses," and were executed either on the spot or
soon thereafter. After land reform was completed in 1952,
agriculture was collectivized through a series of measures

until 1957, when most peasants were persuaded to join co-
operatives. The educated classes were sent to revolutionary
universities to be reeducated, and the recalcitrant were often subjected to brainwashing and sometimes to physical
torture. Churches, political organizations, businesses, and
labor unions all were placed under Communist Party control. A pervasive system of social controls was established in
all neighborhoods.

Political and civil rights, particularly those rights which
are emphasized in the West—such as religious freedom,
freedom of speech and press, equal protection of the law,
and the right to a fair trial under due process—were denied
most Chinese. The Chinese Communist Party, which openly dominated all activities of the state and society, was not
subject to any restraint by law. Western-style democracy
was not put into even temporary practice in China. Elections were rare occurrences, and voting was permitted only
for approved candidates. Opposition from outside the
Communist Party was not tolerated. Almost any questioning of the political system was regarded as a criminal of-
fense.

The Chinese Communists thus restored the authority of
a powerful central state in China. In many ways, Mao Zedong and the CCP substituted Marxism-Leninism for Confucian doctrine. The main features of Marxism fitted in well
with Chinese tradition. In many peasants' eyes, Mao became the new Son of Heaven, and his writings and thoughts
quickly assumed the authority of edicts from an emperor.
The new elite, the Chinese Communist Party cadres,
stepped into the role of the scholar-officials of the past. Selected for their intelligence and loyalty to party doctrine,
they became guardians of the new Communist social order
much as the scholar-officials of the past had protected the
Confucian order. Similarly, the idea that the purpose of an

individual's life was not to express his own personality, but to serve the group was reaffirmed by the Communists. In addition, Marxism was relevant to China's contemporary needs. Confucianism looked to a golden age in the past. Marxism rejected the past and provided the Chinese with a hope of progress toward a golden age in the future. Marxism also enabled the Chinese to condemn the wicked capitalist West, which had humiliated their nation so often. At the same time, though, Marxism also claimed to be an essentially "scientific" system of thought that enabled the CCP to adopt Western science and technology.

All Chinese Communist leaders agreed that modernization and rapid economic growth were necessary to restore China's former greatness. However, there were sharp differences of opinion over how China should modernize. This debate became part of the long-standing dispute over the methods of modernizing China and what role Western countries should play in the process. Mao Zedong stood for the creation of a new China through ideological indoctrination and mass movements. He wanted to level the differences between living conditions in the cities and countryside and to create a classless society in which peasants, workers, and intellectuals would be fused into a single social class. He urged his nation to be self-reliant and to minimize contact with foreign ideas and technology. Other party leaders, including Deng Xiaoping, wanted to raise China's industrial growth rate as quickly as possible by educating technical and managerial experts whose purpose it would be to guide the economy. They thought that skilled workers and intellectuals should be given special treatment and such incentives as better pay and housing, better education, and better medical care. They believed in a rapid rate of economic growth and modernization, even at the expense of egalitarianism and self-reliance.

The history of the People's Republic of China suggests a zigzag pattern of development. China since 1949 has alternated between mass mobilization and industrial development. During the thirty years of its existence Communist China has experimented with many models. In the early 1950s China embarked on its First Five-Year Plan, a strategy based on the Soviet development pattern. China's leaders unleashed an enormous campaign to urge learning from the Soviet Union. Under the slogan "Their today is our tomorrow," China copied in wholesale fashion Russia's state and party institutions, its industry, educational system, military techniques, and strict social controls. Then, in 1956, Mao Zedong decided that Soviet-style restrictions on the free flow of ideas were excessive. He believed that reactionaries and class enemies had been safely eliminated from the political scene in China and that everyone basically accepted the new order. Consequently, he decided that it would be healthy if people could air their views more freely. He called for a period of intellectual freedom, saying, "Let a hundred flowers bloom and a hundred points of view contend." Thus, the campaign came to be called the Hundred Flowers Campaign. At first, people were reluctant to speak out, but in the spring of 1957 attacks on party policy came in torrents. Mao had expected criticism of policies and projects but not general criticism of communism and the government. He was astounded and called the Hundred Flowers "poisonous weeds." He ordered a rectification campaign against intellectuals who had spoken out. Tens of thousands of them were branded as rightists, and many were imprisoned for as long as twenty years or more. Thus, much of the brainpower that could have helped Mao modernize China was lost to him.

By 1957 Mao Zedong had become aware of the limitations of the Soviet pattern of development and had begun to realize that the Russian model was not applicable to Chinese conditions. The major problem with the Soviet plan was that it stressed industrialization at the expense of agriculture. But more than 80 percent of China's population lived in the countryside; therefore, the Chinese had to find a strategy that would foster simultaneous development of both agriculture and industry. Disillusioned with intellectuals, Mao turned to men and women of solid political background to find a "Chinese way" to develop and modernize. They were to lead the public in a Great Leap Forward, in which China would try to overcome formidable economic problems through sheer willpower. Agriculture, which had been collectivized in the early 1950s, was to be reorganized around communes. Thus, through vast work schemes and mass mobilization the party would try to harness all the energies of the people to attain industrialization and self-reliance in as short a time as possible.

Communes all over China did try to increase the production of steel by building rudimentary smelting furnaces, crudely made of clay and bricks. The peasants contributed bits of scrap iron, including their own pots and pans, for these backyard blast furnaces. Unfortunately these measures failed because of inadequate planning, poor understanding of economics, and bad weather. Serious food shortages began to develop, and the Great Leap Forward was criticized as too excessive a measure. In the wake of this failure, more pragmatic and conventional economic measures were adopted in the early 1960s. This time the economic program proved successful, and by the middle of the 1960s the average Chinese was probably more prosperous than he had ever been before.

But Mao Zedong foresaw dangers. China's new attempt at rapid industrialization and the need for specialization had created a number of problems. For example, one result was the growth of special class interests and a lessening of emphasis on the collective spirit. Mao did not want communism to mean simply that people were comfortable and well fed. And he certainly did not want a situation in which the party elite merely filled the same roles once played by the scholar-officials. If that came to pass, in Mao's eyes, there might as well never have been a revolution at all. Fearful that the accomplishments of the Chinese Revolution were in danger of being abandoned, Mao called for a new national political campaign.

The Cultural Revolution of 1966–1969 was inspired by Mao's desire to attack the old order and to eliminate elitism in the educational system and in the bureaucracy. In order to carry out the Cultural Revolution, Mao mobilized many of China's young people as Red Guards. These university and school students were Mao's shock troops. Schools and colleges closed down as students flocked to Beijing on free travel passes. Mao received millions of Red Guards in gigantic parades and symbolically appointed himself their leader by donning their red armband.

The situation was tumultuous. Thousands of Red Guards camped all over the capital, causing shortages of food and other essentials. They tore down street names reminiscent of the old China and replaced them with new ones. Red Guards campaigned against the "four olds": old ideas, old culture, old customs, and old habits. Some broke into houses searching for Buddhist images, old property deeds, jewelry, and other personal belongings dating from the old China. Radical groups even occasionally seized control of government offices, such as the Foreign Ministry, and searched private records for evidence of deviation from the line of Mao Zedong.

The Cultural Revolution was, however, much more than

an opportunity for young people to behave like hoodlums. Its first aim was to transform the educational system. Mao charged that rural children and the poor were being discriminated against in education because the best schools and teachers were reserved for city children and the sons and daughters of party cadres. He also felt that formal education in China was too lengthy and was irrelevant to the needs of the nation. Consequently, he deemed an overhaul necessary and set forth the goals of the educational revolution in a directive in May 1966:

> Students, while taking studies as the main task, should learn other things as well; namely, besides learning literature they must also learn industry, agriculture and military science, and they must also criticize the bourgeois. The duration of the course of study must be shortened and education must be revolutionized. The situation in which bourgeois intellectuals rule our schools cannot be allowed to continue.

In the midst of this turmoil, struggle, and experiment, a new educational system began to take shape. Vocational education was emphasized, and practical subjects were given priority at the expense of more theoretical studies. Most schools had their own plots of land to farm or were connected with factories where students spent hours learning practical skills on the shop floor. Political indoctrination was stressed, and ordinary people rather than educators were given greater responsibility in the operation of the schools.

The universities went through even more radical changes. Entrance examinations were abolished. Instead, students were selected on the basis of class background, political activism, and practical experience. Young people from peasant and worker backgrounds were favored for admission. Professors were held in contempt. Many were unfairly criticized and physically abused in kangaroo courts. At Chinese universities a virtual witch-hunt took place. In Beijing Normal University there were ninety full and assistant professors in 1966. According to Chinese sources, a total of seventy-three were subjected to investigation, and "some twenty-three professors, assistant professors and staff were persecuted to death." Large numbers of individuals were paraded in public with signs around their necks, denounced at mass rallies, placed in jail, or forced to do penal labor. Naturally the role of professors in higher education was substantially reduced. The power to manage universities was left in the hands of three-in-one revolutionary committees, composed of student representatives, revolutionary cadres, and workers. The courses were considerably shortened, and the emphasis on theoretical work and specialization was lessened while that on practical work was stressed.

The second aim of the Cultural Revolution was to eliminate elitism in the bureaucracy. Again, Mao called on Red Guards to eliminate or reeducate "party persons in authority." Party cadres were accused of "carrying out their work in an authoritarian manner, developing a superior attitude to the workers, forming gangs to protect each other, and taking advantage of their position to gain privileges and amenities for themselves." Red Guards spent endless hours interrogating officials, party cadres, and factory managers. More than half the members of the Central Committee of the Chinese Communist Party, which is the ruling body in China, lost their jobs during the Cultural Revolution. Deng Xiaoping himself was attacked, disgraced, and sent into political exile.

In the heat of this mass political campaign, large-scale violations of human rights took place. Violence and abuse of power were rampant. Recent official revelations described how cadres

> violated laws, wantonly abused their powers, bullied and oppressed the masses and encroached on the public's rights in the process of law enforcement. They even detained people arbitrarily and exacted confessions under duress by hanging them up and beating them. Some took bribes to bend the law and held human lives in contempt.

Such excesses also affected economic performance. Most intellectuals and scientists were actually prevented from contributing their skills to the modernization effort. For example, at the Anshan Iron and Steel Corporation, a national model once hailed by Mao Zedong, 13,000 scientists and technicians were hounded out of their research institutions during the Cultural Revolution. In the mining research institute only 4 scientists were allowed to remain as watchmen. In the iron and steel research center, 121 out of 123 engineers and 716 out of 759 technicians were ejected by Maoist radicals. In Liaoning Province, 10,000 scientific and technical personnel and their families were resettled forcibly in the countryside. Understandably, under such circumstances, little real scientific research was done. Graduate programs in all fields were abolished, and many research institutions were turned into production units in factories. The China University of Science and Technology, for instance, the leading center of science education in China, was moved from Beijing to Anhui (Anhwei) Province. There students undertook work-study projects but were deprived of the advantages of interning in Beijing's Academy of Sciences. Millions of high school and college graduates were sent to the countryside to work alongside the peasants. As a result of all this upheaval, it was not surprising that China's economic output fell drastically.

However, the fragmentary evidence that is available about Chinese politics under Mao suggests that totalitarian techniques were not necessarily the only component of government. Mao Zedong did have considerable popular support, particularly during the early years of his rule. Moreover, he was aware that the attitudes and policies of the party would be genuinely accepted only if the Chinese people were convinced that the Communist position was just and correct. Mao sought to mobilize the Chinese people and mold public opinion to the party viewpoint through ideological campaigns and organizations. Although the party always enjoyed absolute control, the Chinese people occasionally were encouraged to raise questions, voice opinions, and criticize defects in the system. Consequently, ever since 1949 there has been tension between centralism and democracy, and the course of politics has alternated between periods of strict, authoritarian party control and periods of toleration of criticism by the people of the government. Nonetheless, it is true to say that during the past thirty years the Chinese Communist Party has favored political control over participation and that most political dissent in China has been severely punished.

In contrast with its restrictions on civil and political liberties, Communist rule in China under Mao provided considerable gains in the promotion of economic, social, and cultural rights. It is important to remember that compared with that in the United States and other industrial nations, the living standard of the Chinese people is still very low and that most people live extremely hard and frugal lives. Nevertheless, it is a significant achievement that the basic needs of most of the people—food, shelter, clothing, medical care, and education—are being met. Wretched poverty had been the accepted lot of the Chinese peasants for 3,000 years. Wild and unpredictable inflation was a dreaded recurrent fact of life before 1949. Although some people are still hungry in China today, the Chinese Communists have effectively curtailed the extremes of fabulous wealth and dire poverty. As a result, there is no widespread mass poverty, hunger, or destitution. This dramatic reduction in the incidence of destitution is the most notable achievement of Maoist China.

By the time the Cultural Revolution officially ended in 1969, many Chinese leaders, particularly Zhou Enlai, had decided that it was necessary to restore party control of China as soon as possible. Alarmed at the drastic fall in economic output as a result of the chaos of the Cultural Revolution, they argued that unless there was a dramatic increase in production, the Revolution in China would fail. They believed that the Chinese people would not sacrifice themselves indefinitely to the collective good without some greater increases in their own living standard. They also believed that large numbers of scientists, technicians, and experts were required to achieve an economic breakthrough. Therefore, they wanted to use financial and material incentives to spur these experts on in their modernization drive. The Maoists disagreed. They wanted to emphasize continued revolution even at the risk of slower rates of economic growth. Thus, the stage was set for a nationwide debate on the Maoist system and for a fierce struggle for leadership in the post-Mao Zedong era.

The Sino-Soviet-
American Triangle

While various factions of the Chinese leadership were struggling for power in China itself, other dramatic shifts in world politics were taking place. During the 1950s, when China and the Soviet Union were allies, the United States developed an obsessive fear of a Sino-Soviet threat of aggression. Then, in the 1960s, détente between the Soviet Union and the United States caused China to fear the specter of Soviet-American collusion. Finally, in the 1970s, China emerged from several years of isolation and began to improve relations with the United States and to oppose the Soviet Union on all fronts. In order to understand China's role in the world, then, it is necessary to examine the dynamics of the triangular relations of the Soviet Union, China, and the United States in our time.

When Mao Zedong took control of China in 1949, few objective quarrels that could not have been resolved through a policy of compromise existed between his government and the United States. But Americans and Chinese each had memories of the other which prevented compromise. More than a century of tragic history made reconciliation difficult. For example, the thrust of the new revolutionary China was anti-Western, and the Chinese remembered the United States as one of the Western powers that had plundered and exploited their ancestors during the nineteenth

130

and early twentieth centuries. Americans, in turn, believed that they had played the role of China's benevolent guardian and that now China had been "lost" to the Communists—as if China had been America's to lose. Ordinary Americans were dismayed and bitterly disappointed to see their generous goodwill of many years' standing washed away by the defeat of the KMT.

International factors were also important. In the same year that the Chinese civil war ended with the Communists' victory, the cold war between the United States and the Soviet Union began in earnest. Despite evidence that Mao Zedong wished to keep his political and economic options open and thus avoid total dependence on the Soviet Union, American leaders saw the Chinese Communist victory in 1949 as proof of Soviet expansionism. Secretary of State Dean Acheson declared that the Chinese Communists were abominable villains who had "forsworn their Chinese heritage and have publicly announced their subservience to a foreign power, Russia. . . ."

Republicans in the U.S. Senate and House became hysterical and used the China issue to attack the Democrats in American politics. Senator Joseph McCarthy of Wisconsin took advantage of the tension and suspicion to carry out an extensive series of investigations. He believed that Mao Zedong and the CCP were the forces of evil and could not and should not be allowed triumph. Thus, McCarthy developed the myth that the United States had "lost" China as a result of the work of subversives in the American government. According to McCarthy, Mao's victory had been the result of a plot directed from Moscow and helped by "traitors" in the American government. Foreign Service officers who had dared criticize Chiang Kai-shek and the KMT were falsely accused of being agents of Moscow and were driven out of the State Department. Many other individuals in the arts and in the film industry were put on blacklists, lost their jobs, and had their reputations and careers ruined by the "Red scare." McCarthy's tactics made it virtually impossible for the Truman administration to come to terms with communism in China. Such action would have meant political suicide for the Democratic Party. Even when the spasm of McCarthyism finally passed, many Americans continued to believe that China had been betrayed by the forces of evil.

The confrontation was by no means only an American creation, for Communist China was set against the United States ideologically, too. To the Chinese Communists, the world was divided into "imperialist" and "oppressed" peoples. Mao Zedong considered the United States the world's leading imperialist power and, as such, China's archenemy. Nor had the Chinese forgotten that the United States had supplied Chiang Kai-shek with several billion dollars in aid for his struggle against the CCP. As a result, America quickly became China's mortal enemy. Shortly after assuming power, the CCP unceremoniously ousted U.S. official representatives from Beijing and seized all American property. In retaliation, the United States stated that it would not recognize the People's Republic of China because the government was not in control of the entire country, was not in accord with the will of its own people, and showed no intention of honoring its international obligations. Americans who once could travel in China freely suddenly found themselves locked out.

The Soviet Union, on the other hand, immediately recognized the People's Republic of China as a legitimate government as well as Mao's right to rule all China. Mao Zedong had declared that the Chinese would "lean to one side" to support the forces of socialism against those of imperialism. In early 1950 Mao Zedong went to Moscow, where he concluded a treaty of military alliance with the Soviet Union. At a time when China was very weak and had no other power to which it could turn, the Sino-Soviet alliance gave the new People's Republic much needed political and military support against the threat of a hostile United States. In spite of tension between Chinese and Soviet Communists and the Soviets' lukewarm support for the Chinese Revolution, Mao accepted Stalin's leadership of the socialist bloc. He praised the achievements of the USSR and declared that China would be rebuilt on the Russian model. The United States feared, above all else, the menace of a monolithic Sino-Soviet bloc. Consequently, when China concluded its treaty of alliance with Russia, it looked to Washington as if China would be little more than a tool of the Russians.

The real turning point in relations between the United States and China occurred when North Korea attacked South Korea in June 1950. American troops were sent as United Nations forces in support of South Korea. More important, President Truman made a series of decisions which fixed the course of U.S. policy in Asia for the next twenty years and transformed America into a full-fledged Pacific power. Truman used the outbreak of fighting in Korea as the occasion to declare that any attack on the Nationalist Chinese forces on Taiwan would be considered to be an attack on the United States. He then ordered the American Seventh Fleet to patrol the Taiwan Strait in order to prevent a Chinese Communist attack. Mao Zedong interpreted these American actions as a direct intervention in the internal affairs of China and as one more example of America's long-standing hostility toward the Chinese Communists.

The world as viewed from Beijing was a picture of unswerving American hostility. China perceived itself as threatened by the United States from three directions. American troops were marching directly up to the Sino-Korean border at the Yalu River. The United States was protecting the hated Chiang Kai-shek regime on Taiwan and was siding with the French who were trying to protect their colonial interests against the Vietnamese revolutionaries in Indochina. In addition, the United States was rebuilding and rearming Japan. Hence, the Chinese leadership reasoned that the intention of the United States was "to make use of Taiwan as a springboard for the invasion of the Chinese mainland. . . . Her plan is to invade China after her complete occupation of Korea." Thus, it was not surprising that China intervened on behalf of North Korea when American forces under General Douglas MacArthur advanced toward the Sino-Korean border. The Korean War dragged on until 1953 and ended in the division of the country into a Communist North Korea and a non-Communist South Korea. The head-on confrontation in Korea resulted in China and America becoming bitter enemies.

For the next twenty years relations between Beijing and Washington were frozen in hostility. The Chinese Communists regarded the United States as China's number one enemy. In American eyes the Soviet Union and China represented a formidable Communist monolith stretching from the banks of the Elbe in Europe to the shores of the Pacific in Asia. Communist forces seemed to menace not only Western Europe but also Japan and the states of Southeast Asia. Americans were convinced that unless firmly held in check, China would try to extend its power all over the Far East. Alarmed by this apparent danger, the United States acted to strengthen America's defenses in Asia. In the years following the Korean conflict, American military alliances were concluded with Japan, South Korea, and Taiwan. In addition, the United States refused to recognize the legitimacy of the Beijing government, blocked China's claim to a seat at the United Nations, imposed a trade embargo and travel bans, and took numerous other hostile actions short of war.

The cold war in Asia continued until the 1970s. The United States continued to view the problem of Chinese power in Asia in much the same light as it saw Soviet power in Europe. Both Beijing and Moscow posed a military and strategic threat. Despite great differences between China and Russia in power and outlook, the United States believed that both nations could be contained or checked by military alliances and the stationing of U.S. troops overseas.

However, the Sino-Soviet alliance was far stormier than most Americans realized. Soviet aid to China was never very generous. Although Stalin had granted several hundred million dollars' worth of credits to Beijing, he insisted that China pay for the almost $1 billion worth of military equipment during the Korean War. Stalin also insisted that the Soviet Union be allowed to keep its special port and railroad privileges in Manchuria. Although after Stalin's death the Russians finally did agree to a more generous aid package and to a complete withdrawal from Manchuria, the Chinese never felt that the Soviets were willing to pass on technological know-how that might increase Chinese independence. Finally, in 1959, Chinese fears were confirmed when the Soviet Union reneged on a pledge to assist China in acquiring a nuclear capability.

Mao also believed that Moscow must eventually come to accept the Chinese as full partners in the Communist movement and admit that the Chinese political and economic model of development was applicable to other developing nations. Mao's disastrous Great Leap Forward in 1958 was understood by both parties to be a Chinese declaration of independence from the Soviet model and a questioning of Russia's prerogative to lead the Communist movement. Consequently, from 1958 on the Chinese could claim that Mao had added new truths to the Marxist canon. Old Chinese feelings of superiority resurfaced. Beijing argued that China rather than Russia should be the model for less developed countries to follow.

Political and ideological disputes further widened the rift between the Soviet Union and the People's Republic of China. Stalin's successor, Nikita Khrushchev, advocated détente and peaceful coexistence with the United States. But according to the Chinese, this Russian line betrayed Chinese interests and the long-term goals of world revolution.

Soviet responses to military threats against the Chinese further damaged the Sino-Soviet alliance. During both the Korean War and the Taiwan Strait crisis of 1958 the United States had threatened to use nuclear weapons against China. In Korea, Russia had given China arms and equipment but no troops. During the Taiwan Strait crisis, Soviet support dwindled to halfhearted verbal warnings against direct American intervention. Finally, in the Chinese war with India in 1962, the Soviet Union actually supplied the Indians with military and economic aid to fight the Chinese. Russian reluctance to support China when its security interests were at stake made Mao Zedong question the value of the Sino-Soviet alliance.

Relations between the two Communist giants grew more and more hostile. By the early 1960s Khrushchev had withdrawn all Soviet aid to China and broken off party relations between the two states. Incidents along the Sino-Soviet border in Central and East Asia began in 1962. The 4,500-mile boundary between the two states was poorly marked, and even in the best of times each side accused the other of planning to seize more land along the common border. Violent polemics between Moscow and Beijing increased as the border disputes became more frequent and intense. Because China had national interests different from those of the Soviet Union and refused to act as a subordinate, the Soviets tried to expel China from the international Communist movement. The Chinese government, in turn, regarded the Russian leaders as "new czars," who bullied China and other countries.

During the 1960s China felt increasingly isolated by the lack of Soviet support and threatened by the American military buildup in Vietnam and other parts of Asia. Although China and Russia were by this time in open dispute, the American stand against China remained rigid. Surprisingly there was no Western initiative to profit from the Sino-Soviet conflict. On the contrary, American participation in the war in Vietnam brought the two powers to the brink of a disastrous conflict.

The enduring hostility was not solely a product of the years of Sino-Soviet alliance. During the chaotic period of the Cultural Revolution, China became almost completely isolated from the international community and adopted a radical position in world affairs. While isolating itself, Beijing nonetheless encouraged "wars of national liberation" in the underdeveloped world, especially in Asia. Because the Chinese had successfully used guerrilla warfare against the Nationalists and Japanese, they believed that the same kind of warfare could be employed by revolutionary groups in Asia, Africa, and Latin America. Principally through propaganda and moral support, but also by helping train revolutionary cadres, the Chinese encouraged revolution in other countries. In some countries, such as Vietnam, and in Africa and the Middle East, they even provided arms to revolutionaries. However, China was not prepared to risk direct involvement in another country's revolution by providing Chinese troops or cadres. The Chinese believe that "wars of national liberations" must rely primarily on the resources of the local people.

By the late 1960s several important shifts in global politics had begun to bring China out of its isolation and to modify its radical foreign policy posture. First, the Soviet Union rather than the United States had become China's principal enemy. When, in August 1968, the Soviet Union invaded a fraternal Communist state, Czechoslovakia, in order to depose an increasingly independent socialist regime, alarm bells went off in Beijing. The Soviet action confirmed Mao Zedong's belief that Russia had aggressive intentions toward any Communist state that strayed from Moscow's leadership. Then, in March 1969, Chinese and Soviet armed forces clashed along disputed parts of the Sino-Soviet border. Both nations began to move large military forces into the region, and the USSR threatened China with possible nuclear war.

While Chinese relations with the Soviets deteriorated, Chinese-American relations clearly improved. With the beginning of the American disengagement in Vietnam Beijing believed the U.S. government might finally be willing to come to realistic terms with the Chinese Communists. The United States, for its part, hoped that it could exploit the Sino-Soviet split to play Moscow and Beijing off against each other. Consequently, in 1971, the United States cleared the way for negotiations with China by agreeing eventually to withdraw its military forces from Taiwan and to leave the Chinese Nationalists to settle their differences with Beijing as an internal affair. With this agreement, the two countries moved cautiously toward rapprochement. Also in 1971, the United Nations voted, 76 to 35, to admit the People's Republic of China and expel the representatives of Chiang Kai-shek's government on Taiwan. Thus, China finally became a member of the United Nations with a permanent seat on the Security Council. After President Richard Nixon's visit to the China in early 1972, contacts at many levels short of formal recognition were established, and the possibilities of trade and exchange programs were explored. For the first time in a quarter of a century face-to-face contacts between the peoples of China and America became possible. A relationship that had been based for an entire generation on fiction, anxiety, and fear showed signs of returning to reality.

This cautious progress continued after Mao Zedong's death in 1976. The new Chinese leadership continued to look to America and the West for security against the Soviet Union and for economic and technological help in the drive toward modernization. To promote U.S.-China trade and to improve political relations, the United States established full diplomatic relations with the People's Republic of China and granted China most-favored-nation trade status in 1979. At the same time the United States broke off official relations and terminated its security treaty with the Republic of China on Taiwan. Since then, tensions across the Taiwan Strait have been greatly reduced. The Chinese Communists have begun to report objectively on Taiwan cultural affairs, and although there is still no official China-Taiwan trade, the trade which always took place through Hong Kong has become more open.

While discouraging the Chinese from relying too heavily on capitalist foreign countries and losing their national pride, China's new leaders recognize the need for foreign technology and managerial expertise. They realize that to bring about modernization rapidly, China must import large quantities of sophisticated and expensive technology from the West and Japan. Because it simply does not have the foreign exchange to buy these goods, Beijing will have to borrow money from the West. There is, however, still disagreement within the Chinese Communist leadership on whether to go deeply into debt to buy technology from the former Western imperialist powers. There is also doubt about the wisdom of transferring massive technology from the West at the expense of self-reliance. There is also the danger that given China's primarily agricultural economy, the nation will not be able to absorb the inflow of sophisticated technology fast enough. Recognizing these dangers, Chinese economic planners have recently conceded that China must proceed more slowly. Under their new plan, the Chinese will focus on improving agricultural and light industrial production at the expense of heavy industry in order to raise the living standard of the people more rapidly. For the most part they will probably use a combination of self-help and limited foreign aid to improve what they already have. This retrenchment has disappointed enterprising Western traders who dream of opening up the vast China market. Their euphoria has been supplanted by a more sober and realistic view of China's economic potential during the remainder of the twentieth century.

10

New Directions under Deng Xiaoping

Beginning in the early 1970s, party leaders such as Deng Xiaoping and Zhou Enlai tried to reverse the damage done to the economy during the Cultural Revolution and to inspire a concern for law and order. They believed that if China wished to make life better and more prosperous for its people, it must embark on programs of rapid industrialization and technological advancement. Adopting the slogan "Strive for four modernizations," they maintained that China's main economic objective should be to reach advanced world standards in agriculture, industry, science and technology, and national defense by the year 2000.

The drive to restore economic growth soon fell victim to further political discontent and disintegration. During the final illnesses of Mao Zedong and Zhou Enlai in 1975 and 1976, political strife between Deng Xiaoping and the Maoist radicals intensified. Shortly after the death of Mao his widow, Jiang Qing, and the rest of the radicals, the so-called Gang of Four, were arrested and disgraced in public. Their supporters were also purged, jailed, or executed. Mao Zedong was criticized for having become isolated from the people in his later years. Deng Xiaoping was formally reinstated as a senior party leader in 1977, and in 1978 the nation was ordered by the Chinese Communist Party to return to a policy of constitutional and economic transformation.

Under Deng Xiaoping, the reforms of the Cultural Revolution have been almost completely dismissed and criticized. In 1978 Deng pushed ahead with the Four Modernizations program and launched a series of sweeping reforms designed to refashion Chinese Communism according to his own ideals. Perhaps the most notable of Deng's decisions has been to involve foreign countries on a large scale in China's modernization. A liberal foreign investment code has been adopted to encourage outsiders to set up business in China. Because China needs qualified scientists, technicians, and managers immediately, the Chinese government has also drawn up plans to send large numbers of its best students abroad to study. During the past ten years thousands of Chinese students have been sent to Japan, Western Europe, the United States, and Australia to study science and technology. In contrast with Mao's preference for isolation from outside contact, Deng insists that China must learn from other nations. He has stated: "Independence does not mean shutting the door on the world nor does self-reliance mean blind opposition to everything foreign. Science and technology are a kind of wealth created in common by all mankind." In the century-old debate over the appropriate path for China to take to achieve modernization, Deng sides with the Self-Strengthening Movement of the nineteenth century and the May Fourth Movement of the twentieth century. Their emphasis on science, technology, and Western learning as the answer to China's problems and the key to its modernization is largely in line with Deng's views.

Material incentives have also been reintroduced to get people to return to hard work and productivity after the disruptions caused by the Cultural Revolution. Former businessmen and industrialists, whose businesses were seized during the Maoist era, have been paid large sums of money by the Chinese government as compensation and incentive to return to work. Industrial workers are receiving cash bonuses for hard work and good output. In rural areas, peasants are again free to farm their private plots and to sell the produce on the free market. Along with the introduction of incentives has come the setting up of an income tax program, the first in China since the Communists came to power in 1949.

Most important, a new constitution that reestablished legal guarantees and some minimal protection of basic human rights was drawn up in 1978. The constitution grants to Chinese citizens the right to freedom of expression, fair trials, and full defenses against charges made. Chinese officials have repeatedly stated that the courts and their strict regard for the law are the front line of defense against bad government and the abuse of human rights. However, many Chinese remain skeptical about the significance of the new laws. After what they have experienced, the Chinese, more than most people, know that the law on the books is one thing and the law in action may be quite different. The lack of adequate legal protections given the defendants in the Gang of Four trial in 1980 confirmed these fears in the minds of many people.

To emphasize further the need for free discussion, the Chinese government allowed and even encouraged criticism and demands for human rights during a brief period in the winter of 1978–79. However, in a speech early in 1980, Deng Xiaoping made quite clear what modernization meant to him. It concerned industry, agriculture, and science and technology. Human rights figured only to the extent that greater freedom for intellectuals would enable China to advance its national goals. Deng stated clearly that political stability must take precedence over freedom of expression. Alluding to the Cultural Revolution, he noted: "We suffered for more than ten years in the past, and the people will not and cannot tolerate any more turmoil." In his view, human rights are meaningful only if they serve the purpose of the Communist Party or economic growth. Thus, newspapers may continue to print criticism of the government, but it must always be constructive. And while the Communist Party should not interfere with artists and writers, the artists must remember that their works should "serve the interests of the people, the state and the party." Deng was particularly scornful of the "so-called democrats and dissidents" who put up posters on Beijing's Democracy Wall. In response to their activities, he stated: "At present some people doubt the socialist system and babble that socialism is inferior to capitalism. We must correct this idea forcefully." Deng apparently believes that the party must demonstrate firmness in its resolve to achieve modernization without being an intolerable tyranny.

Deng's plan to foster a new intellectual elite, to rely extensively on foreign trade and technology, and to employ material incentives to promote China's modernization program makes good economic sense. However, rapid economic growth will necessarily have considerable political and social consequence for China. There is a danger that the already sizable gap between urban and rural living standards will be widened further. Rapid industrialization is most likely to benefit those who live in the cities, thus arousing resentment in the great mass of Chinese people who earn their living from the land. Moreover, under Deng, the party and the government have maintained the rigid division of Chinese society into the masses and the bureaucratic elite, with its privileges and immunities. Senior party and state officials, senior army officers, and industrial managers have luxuries unknown to most Chinese. They have the use of limousines and lavish country homes. Many of them live in special blocks of apartments reserved for cadres. Their children go to special schools, find the jobs they want, and generally advance more quickly in life. They are provided with special hospitals and stores and have access to films and literature not available to ordinary citizens.

This was the very system of privilege and inequalities that the Cultural Revolution was designed to shake up. Mao Zedong appealed over the heads of the party to students, workers, and peasants to root out corrupt officials, overthrow the party bureaucracy, and set up, instead, revolutionary committees comprising workers, peasants, and soldiers to run the factories and communes. However, when the Cultural Revolution got completely out of control, masses of innocent people were persecuted, and the economy was severely disrupted. As a consequence, Deng and others have totally repudiated the Cultural Revolution, and many of its more worthwhile aspects have been overturned in the process. For example, the reintroduction of examinations as the sole means of entry into higher education has effectively excluded most children of workers and peasants from colleges and universities.

There is also some question whether the stress on quality, elitism, and academic achievement will solve the problems of education or generally meet China's needs. At the current stage of its development China's needs are more those of a developing country than of a developed one. For example, there are still substantial differences between the incomes of urban and rural peoples. Those who live and work in the cities earn on average twice as much as those who toil in the countryside. Despite Mao's attempts during the Cultural Revolution to narrow the gap between urban and rural living standards, housing, education, and health care are still both of higher quality and more available in the cities than in the country. Moreover, neither hunger nor illiteracy has been completely eliminated. Even greater than the difference between city and country, however, is the difference between rich and poor provinces. China's wealth lies along the coast. As one travels inland, agriculture becomes less productive and the standard of living drops. There are considerable variations in rural income both between and within provinces in the countryside. Rural communes closer to the cities are far richer than communes in more remote areas of the countryside.

China's economy consists of a large, relatively backward agricultural sector and a small but expanding, modern urban one. Most jobs are in the agricultural sector and require a low level of education or technical training. Thus, what China needs, in the short run, is a small number of highly trained specialists to lead its modernization effort and a much larger number of people with less education to serve in the agricultural sector and help spread knowledge of modern technology there. Only as the country modernizes will the need for highly trained specialists gradually increase. The current educational emphasis, however, aims at turning out more highly trained specialists and fewer low-level technicians than needed. In fact, as a result of the stress on higher education, the Chinese school system very likely will turn out more highly trained and educated people than the economy, at its current stage of development, can absorb. The majority of Chinese youth, therefore, will continue to have to work either in the countryside or in unattractive jobs in the cities. Yet the current educational program fails to prepare most students for this prospect. The result may very well be a class of overqualified, alienated intellectuals for whom no appropriate jobs are available.

Other costs and risks associated with Deng's modernization program include the almost inevitable failure of the standard of living to keep pace with the rising expectations. Hoping to gain real benefits from the modernization program, workers and peasants are demanding higher pay and a higher standard of living. This surge of expectations, however, is taking place at the very time when the need for increased investment in industry and agriculture rules out immediate significant improvement in the income of most Chinese.

In spite of the disrepute in which his programs are held today, Mao Zedong in many ways correctly diagnosed a number of China's problems. He foresaw the danger of increasing social inequalities, the problems of creating an overeducated, overqualified elite, and the need for people whose talents and training are suited to China's agricultural economy. The problem Deng Xiaoping must now address is how to modernize without increasing frustrations and social tensions in the country.

In addition, although there is wide support for most of Deng's reform measures, the Chinese government still faces an uphill battle in trying to implement them. The most immediate problem is the continued opposition to reform from supporters of Maoist policies. Most of the opposition comes from middle- and lower-level cadres who rose to their positions of authority during the Cultural Revolution. The younger cadres are genuinely opposed on ideological grounds to Deng's pragmatic and un-Maoist policies, but they are also understandably reluctant to rehabilitate the veteran officials whom they ousted and replaced during the Cultural Revolution. They stand to lose out under the new system. Their opposition will probably continue for some time and will slow the implementation of new policies. Also, the army is reportedly upset by cuts in the military budget and by its low position in China's modern-

ization program. The army's prestige among the people has
fallen in recent years, and the four-million-strong People's
Liberation Army is increasingly restive over its loss of political power, and over Beijing's recent pragmatic course.

Related to Maoist opposition are low morale, apathy, and
skepticism among large numbers of intellectuals, students,
and educators. Many of these people were purged during
the Cultural Revolution for supporting policies similar to
those being implemented now. Because of their experi-
ences, they are reluctant to support the new reforms openly for fear that the party line might change and they would
once again be persecuted for their views. Many Chinese intellectuals no longer believe what their leaders tell them.
They have seen too many abrupt changes in the party line
over the past two decades. To take the most obvious example, over the past fifteen years the Chinese people have
been led to believe that Deng Xiaoping was good, then bad,
then good, then bad, and, finally, good again. Or take the
case of Liu Shaoqi. During the early 1960s he was the respected president of China, but during the Cultural Revolution he was accused of having been an agent of the
Japanese in the 1930s. Recently he has been posthumously
rehabilitated as one of the great leaders of the Chinese Revolution. Other examples abound. One day Lin Biao (Lin
Piao) was Mao's "trusted comrade-in-arms," and the next
he was a "renegade and traitor." Yesterday Chairman Mao
and the Gang of Four could do no wrong. Today they are
blamed for everything that has gone sour in China in recent
years. The rise and fall of each leader have been accompanied by a political campaign designed to provide each turn
of events with a basis consistent with Marxist-Leninist principles. It is no small wonder that faced with such abrupt
changes in the party line, many people in China simply
choose to remain silent, chant the political slogan of the

elite currently in power, and hope for the best. Party policies have not generated the mass enthusiasm necessary for a successful modernization drive.

Skepticism about the durability of Deng's modernization program remains strong within China. Just as Mao failed because he overemphasized the possibility of modernizing China through mass mobilization and underemphasized the need to combat human rights violations by developing institutions that could check the abuse of power and privilege, so, too, Deng may fail because he could not persuade the Chinese people to participate fully in the modernization effort without offering them a good measure of political freedom. Given the cyclical pattern of politics and social change in recent Chinese history, the country will probably have only a short period of relative political stability in which to demonstrate the efficacy of Deng's modernization program. If it can be shown that current modernization policies work to improve the national economy and raise the standard of living, then the leadership of Deng Xiaoping and Zhao Ziyang will be vindicated. If results are not forthcoming, then a resurgence of instability and Maoist radicalism may threaten China's modernization effort. To be successful in the long term, China must satisfy both the material and the spiritual needs of its people. According to a Chinese dissident, "man does not live by material things alone; he needs more political freedom, too."

In the next few years China's leadership may change again, but the policy debate over which road China should take to modernize will certainly continue. Will the government put money into industry or continue to give priority to agriculture? Will the government make higher education available to the masses or concentrate its meager resources on the intellectually gifted to develop a managerial elite? Will the party relax its restrictions to allow for a more open society or clamp down on opposition forces when they threaten party control? Will China rely on its own efforts to modernize or adapt wholeheartedly from the Western industrial countries?

Complex changes are taking place in this ancient country. But one thing is clear. China is determined to develop from a relatively poor country to a modern superpower. The price to be paid will be enormous, and success will depend on whether the leadership can achieve the Mandate of Heaven in the eyes of the people.

Bibliography

Amnesty International. *Report on Political Imprisonment in the People's Republic of China.* London: Amnesty International Publications, 1978.

Beeching, Jack. *The Chinese Opium Wars.* New York: Harcourt Brace Jovanovich, 1975.

Belden, Jack. *China Shakes the World.* New York: Monthly Review Press, 1970. Penguin Books, 1973.

Buchanan, Keith. *The Chinese People and the Chinese Earth.* London: G. Bell and Sons, 1966.

Ch'en, Jerome. *Mao.* Englewood Cliffs, New Jersey: Prentice-Hall, 1969.

Clubb, O. Edmund. *Twentieth Century China.* New York: Columbia University Press, 1978.

Dawson, Raymond. *The Chinese Chameleon.* London: Oxford University Press, 1967.

———. *The Legacy of China.* London: Oxford University Press, 1971.

Davies, John Paton. *Dragon by the Tail.* New York: Norton, 1972.

Fairbank, John K. *The United States and China.* Cambridge, Massachusetts: Harvard University Press, 1971.

———, Edwin O. Reischauer, and Albert Craig. *East Asia: Tradition and Transformation.* Boston: Houghton Mifflin, 1973.

Fitzgerald, Charles P. *The Chinese View of Their Place in the World.* New York: Oxford University Press, 1969.

———. *Communism Takes China.* New York: American Heritage Press, 1971.

Gittings, John. *A Chinese View of China.* New York: Pantheon Books, 1973.

Hart, Robert A. *The Eccentric Tradition: American Diplomacy in the Far East.* New York: Charles Scribner's Sons, 1976.

Hinton, William. *Fanshen: A Documentary of Revolution in a Chinese Village.* New York: Vintage Books, 1968.

Hookham, Hilda. *A Short History of China.* London: Longman, 1969.

Isaacs, Harold. *Scratches on Our Minds: American Images of India and China.* New York: John Day and Co., 1958.

Langer, William. *The Diplomacy of Imperialism.* New York: Knopf, 1935.

Leys, Simon. *Chinese Shadows.* New York: Penguin, 1978.

Loescher, Gil and Ann Dull. *The Chinese Way.* New York: Harcourt Brace Jovanovich, 1974.

McClellan, Robert. *The Heathen Chinese: A Study of American Attitudes Towards China, 1890–1905.* Columbus: Ohio State University Press, 1971.

McNair, Harley Farnsworth. *Modern Chinese History, Selected Readings.* Shanghai: Shanghai Commercial Press Ltd., 1923.

Miller, Stuart. *The Unwelcome Immigrant: American Images of the Chinese, 1785–1882.* Berkeley: University of California Press, 1969.

Milton, David, and Nancy Milton, eds. *The China Reader Four—People's China: Social Experimentation, Politics, Entry onto the World Scene, 1966–1972.* New York: Random House, 1974.

Myrdal, Jan, and Gun Kessle. *China: The Revolution Con-*

tinued. New York: Random House, 1970.

————. *Chinese Journey.* New York: Random House, 1965.

————. *Report from a Chinese Village.* New York: New American Library, 1965.

Needham, Joseph. *Science and Civilization in China.* London: Cambridge University Press, 1964.

————. *Within the Four Seas: The Dialogue of East and West.* London: George Allen and Unwin, 1969.

Newnham, Richard, and Tan Lin-tung. *About Chinese.* London: Penguin Books, 1971.

Oksenberg, Michael C., et al. *A Bibliography of Secondary English Language Literature on Contemporary Chinese Politics.* New York: East Asia Institute, Columbia University, 1970.

Pepper, Suzanne. *Civil War in China: The Political Struggle, 1945–1949.* Berkeley: University of California Press, 1978.

Posner, Arlene, and Arne J. de Keijzer, eds. *China: A Resource and Curriculum Guide.* Chicago: University of Chicago Press, 1973.

Pye, Lucian W. *China: An Introduction.* Boston: Little Brown and Co., 1972.

Schaller, Michael. *The United States and China in the Twentieth Century.* New York: Oxford University Press, 1979

————. *The United States Crusade in China, 1938–1945.* New York: Columbia University Press, 1979.

Schram, Stuart. *Mao Tse-tung.* New York: Pelican Books, 1967.

Schurmann, Franz, and Orville Schell, eds. *The China Reader.* 3 vols., including *Imperial China, Republican China,* and *Communist China.* New York: Random House, 1967.

Siedel, Ruth. *Women and Child Care in China.* New York:

Farrar, Straus and Giroux, 1972.

Service, John S. *Lost Chance in China: The World War II Dispatches of John S. Service.* New York: Random House, 1974.

Sewell, William G. *I Stayed in China.* Cranbury, New Jersey: A. S. Barnes, 1966.

Snow, Edgar. *The Long Revolution.* New York: Random House, 1972.

————. *Red China Today: The Other Side of the River,* rev. ed. New York: Random House, 1971.

————. *Red Star Over China,* rev. ed. New York: Grove Press, 1968.

Ssu-yu Teng and John Fairbank. *China's Response to the West: A Documentary Survey,* New York: Atheneum, 1971.

Stoessinger, John. *Nations in Darkness: China, Russia, and America.* New York: Random House, 1978.

Tang Tsou. *America's Failure in China.* Chicago: University of Chicago Press, 1963.

White, Theodore, ed. *The Stilwell Papers.* New York: W. Sloane Associates, 1948.

————, and Annalee Jacoby. *Thunder Out of China.* New York: W. Sloane Associates, 1946.

Whiting, Allen S., and Robert F. Dernberger. *China's Future: Foreign Policy and Economic Development.* New York: McGraw-Hill, 1977.

Wilson, Dick. *Anatomy of China: An Introduction to One Quarter of Mankind.* New York: Mentor Books (New American Library), 1969.

Index

155